RICHARD VARNELL BOOK SUMMARY

This book shows pastors of plateaued or declining churches how to develop a first-time guest retention program that results in measurable growth in attendance. This is accomplished through an understanding of biblical principles and sound business strategies.

Richard has pastored churches in Blythe, CA (1968–1963) and Bloomington, CA (1975–1985). He has served the Southern California Assemblies of God Network as both presbyter and executive presbyter. He is the founding President of the Southern California Assemblies of God Founders Fund, which he served from 1998 to 2006. As president, he assisted hundreds of people in preparing Christian wills. He also helped individuals with their investments bringing in $45 million in assets under management.

ENDORSEMENTS FOR
LET YOUR CHURCH GROW

"In a personal and warm style, Richard Varnell renders insights to biblical principles for leaders of churches where growth is deficient and new life is lacking. He covers the landscape of church life and offers practical instruction in navigating the waters of mediocrity. *Let Your Church Grow* is an insightful and helpful guide."

—**Everett Stenhouse**, Assistant General Superintendent,
Assemblies of God (1985-1993)

"This book is captivating and is a well-written account of how Jesus wants us to grow a church. *Let Your Church Grow* gives hope to struggling churches everywhere. You can see the passion for growing a healthy church. A wonderful formula for church growth."

—**Reverend Christopher James Woolley,**
Senior Pastor of Christian Life Church, Canfield,
Ohio & Assistant Presbyter, Greater Youngstown/Warren area network

"Richard has really captured the essence of the working model in ink. *Let Your Church Grow* is easy to read, easy to understand, and easy to implement. This is the 'coaches handbook of church growth' for pastors. Richard lays out each individual piece as well as the whole game plan, making it a simple matter to utilize these tools and see the results. Whether used completely or in part, the results will always be growth. Richard has heart and dedication to the ministry of our Lord, Jesus."

—**Chris Carrigan**, Executive Pastor, Church Planter, Senior Pastor, Interim Pastor, Church Training & Support Ministry

"Church growth is a much-discussed topic with a vast array of talking points. All too often, limited perspective hinders in-depth understanding. *Let Your Church Grow* offers solid research, personal experience, and proven strategies that leave the reader with action steps that are doable. Rather than focusing his efforts on the visionary dreams of new church plants, Richard Varnell focuses his attention on an existing resource with huge possibilities. If we can revitalize the 60 percent of American churches which are declining or plateaued, we can revitalize the influence of the Church in our nation's communities. If you want to hear a compelling case for why your church can grow, that is rooted in biblical foundations and implemented by common sense steps of action, I highly recommend *Let Your Church Grow*."

—**Dr. Byron D. Klaus**, President, Assemblies of God Theological Seminary (1999–2015)

"In *Let Your Church Grow*, Richard Varnell gives proven methods of how ANY and EVERY church can increase their attendance. His ministerial and business background are combined to share specific ideas that, if applied, will result in an older, established church, or a new church plant, experiencing growth. He **guarantees** his methods will work. Try them and put him to the test!"

—**John Heide,** U.S. Missionary to the Second-Half Generations

"I love this kind of book! It's a combination of academic rigor and practical experience while being easy and fun to read. I believe this book will be a great encouragement to pastors and leaders of small churches who want to see their church grow."

—**Dr. Dave Johnson**, Former evangelist and church planter, Faculty member at Asia Pacific Theological Seminary, Managing editor of the *Asian Journal of Pentecostal Studies*

"*Let Your Church Grow* is not only an easy read but makes so much sense. It's biblically based, culturally sensitive, and applying the principles are within easy reach of any congregation, small or large. The unfortunate thing with many congregations which are on a downward slope is getting the people to realize that continuing what they are doing will only bring the same results. This is where the challenge of traditions comes to light. What must remain and what can we change for the good? *Let Your Church Grow* will inspire leaders, as it will give them a sense of direction from someone who has proven that these steps to growth really work."

—**George Smith**, Pastor for more than fifty years

"Many churches today find themselves either plateaued or declining in attendance. Richard Varnell's book, *Let Your Church Grow*, is a practical guide for those desiring to see growth and experience community impact in their local context. Effective steps and resources are identified that will serve as a template for expanding your church's influence both inside and outside of the four walls. I am confident that this book will encourage any reader who is serious about taking their church to a new level."

—**John E. Johnson**, Assistant Superintendent, SoCal Network Assemblies of God

"Richard Varnell's book, *Let Your Church Grow*, is an amazing handbook on a subject about which many others have written, yet it is fresh and challenging. It is powerful because it is loaded with biblical principles, personal experiences, and anecdotes (both his own and those of many others, as the bibliography shows), business principles and technological applications, statistics, and compassion (for kids, single moms, and all first-time guests, for example). Above all, it is practical, practical, practical! These are not just good ideas—they work! Varnell says it best: 'This book is designed to give you hope!' We started church-planting and pastoring fifty years ago in the

U.S. and later in Latin America and the Caribbean. Although God has blessed those efforts, I only wish someone had made this kind of resource available to us at the beginning. Surely it would have enhanced our efforts. I hope before long it can be translated and produced in Spanish for Latin America. I know this book will be a valuable tool for hundreds of struggling pastors and congregations who just need some help to grow as God has designed the church to grow!"

—**Richard Nicholson**, Missionary with Assemblies of God World Missions, Former Regional Director for Latin America & the Caribbean AGWM

"Dr. Varnell's study is an effective research plan to help the average church in America achieve maximum success in visitor reach and retention. His methods are tangible tasks for any leader to perform. Our church has implemented many ideas in this book and has quadrupled our attendance over the last five years. This book is worth a read and deserving of kingdom motivated action."

John Follnow MDiv, Lead Pastor, 3D Palm Assembly of God

"As a current pastor of a small church, and as someone who has been involved in larger ministry contexts, I found the book by Richard Varnell an encouraging reminder to revisit some of the basics of church growth. Having implemented many of the suggestions offered by Richard in previous pastoring venues, I can attest to the fact that such strategies work to build church attendance. The poignant principle of which I was reminded was the importance of being intentionally hospitable to first-time guests to church services and events. Although I, as the pastor, may discern the importance of making guests feel welcome, this is something that needs to be cultivated in the DNA of the members of the church as well. Training in what this will look like in our particular context of ministry must be provided on a regular basis. My intention is to share this book with other key members of our congregation to encourage ownership of some of the implementation of ideas offered herein."

—**Richard Coffelt,** North County Christian Center,
Castroville, California, Senior Pastor

"When I landed in the jungle of my first pastorate, I needed this book. It is a carefully designed blueprint for pastors and churches of less than two hundred. Richard Varnell, an ordained pastor, provides the sound biblical basis for church growth. As a tax consultant, he articulates practical business concepts that help a church measure its goals and be accountable. The book is destined to be a standard for small churches."

—**Dr. Dan Myers**, President, Master Plan Ministries.

"After reading your wonderful book titled, *Let Your Church Grow,* I was encouraged by each chapter as you gave new insights on how to grow a church. I'm convinced that if a leader reads this book and asks the Holy Spirit for guidance, God will ignite the fire in their heart that will burn bright for the ministry of their church.

Perhaps a pastor may feel immobilized by the challenges he faces each week in his church. He may feel paralyzed, and this feeling keeps him from moving forward. Ultimately, he knows he is not living to the fullness and freedom in the ministry that God intends for him; therefore, this book is a must read.

"This book is all about experiencing the power of Christ in your life, to live in victory and have the passion with enthusiasm once again for your Ministry. Each session will equip you with practical, and hands-on step-by-step church growth principles that will take your ministry to a new level of growth in your church."

—**Johnny Gomez**, Associate Pastor, Southcoast Christian
Assembly of God, San Juan Capistrano, California

"After years of both being a pastor and teaching leadership to other pastors, I find that one of the most difficult tasks in the local church is to meaningfully engage first-time guests and then follow through effectively. Richard Varnell, a trusted friend, has done us a wonderful service by addressing this challenge directly and practically. In *Let Your Church Grow*, you will be coached on core systems that will markedly enhance your church's capacity to grow."

—**Dr. James T. Bradford**, General Secretary,
The General Council of the Assemblies of God

"This book will give you practical ways of growing your church from scratch. Whether you are looking to plant a church or revitalize one, you will be encouraged as if you were sitting with your coach. Study what is in this book and then lead yourself and your team toward numeric church growth."

—**Anthony S. Gambino**, Lead Pastor,
Crossroads Assembly of God, Hamburg, New Jersey

"Richard Varnell writes not only as one who has studied church growth but as one who has practiced it. This book would be especially helpful to the pastor and members of smaller churches who are overwhelmed and often discouraged by the beyond-the-reach concepts and models presented by megachurches. His book gives a well-focused application to what a church can do to utilize the potential of its members in a simple but effective manner that will produce results and, therefore, enhance further investment in the church's growth. It will also give new members a sense of belonging to something that is on the move."

—**Greg Austring,** PhD, Former missionary and pastor,
presently teaches missions and intercultural studies,
Vanguard University of Southern California

"*Let Your Church Grow* shares:
- How to recognize God's plan for your church to grow.
- How to overcome anything that would hold your church back from achieving your dream of growth.

- Things you can do to retain first-time guests and to see your church grow.

"Each chapter in *Let Your Church Grow* will help every pastor; church leader, and volunteer identify tangible and 'fixable' dynamics hindering guest retention. This book is well researched and well written. *Let Your Church Grow* contains invaluable information every pastor, regardless of the size of the congregation, can employ in helping retain the first-time guest. This book is a must read for every pastor!"

—**Pastor Fred R. Rodriguez**, Lead Pastor,
Lake Elsinore First Assembly of God, Executive Presbyter,
Southern California Network of the Assemblies of God

"Richard has captured the essence of a growing church; people equipped to love God and care for other people. As he states, 'People are a gift from God.' Through his book *Let Your Church Grow,* Richard is a gift to us, the local pastor. He's a man of optimism and passion to see churches be effective in reaching and retaining the newcomer. This book is an anthology of practical wisdom for the church to serve the newcomer. It surprises you with golden nuggets of practical ideas throughout the text. You'll need two highlighters."

—**Ronn Hobbs**, Lead Pastor, Christian Center,
Desert Hot Springs, California

"In his book, *Let Your Church Grow,* Richard Varnell's business acumen lends itself to some sage advice that is applied through his pastoral calling. He targets the majority of churches in this book with a specific, detailed plan that has been tested and tried and can be emulated. He has gathered a valuable collection of helpful church growth ideas that are all contained in his well-thought-out plan. Richard gives a lot of attention in this book to the very important subjects in church growth of assimilation and turning first-time guests into second-time attenders."

—**Keith Short,** Pastor, Former Presbyter of the Desert Section, Southern California Network Assemblies of God

"I found this book, *Let Your Church Grow,* written by Richard Varnell to be very thorough, precise, and engaging! This book is filled with dynamic possibilities of realized church growth tested by time, efforts, and true wisdom. As a small church pastor, I am encouraged by Richard's passion and guidance to help us use our God-given potential through specific purposed strategies to help grow our churches. I am left with a desire of 'Let's do this for Jesus!'"

—**Anthony Martinez**, Lead Pastor, Olive Branch Assembly of God, Hemet, California

"I always enjoy and appreciate reading books and stories about people who reflect honestly on their work. Richard Varnell has written a compelling story about his work as a pastor/leader. I had the privilege of observing his selfless initiative in planting a wonderful congregation in the greater Palm Springs area. The church grew and thrived as a result of his thoughtful and spiritually focused pastoral leadership. His principles for growing a congregation are sound and meaningful, and offer insight to anyone called to serve Christ's Church."

—**Ray Rachels,** Executive Presbyter, General Council Assemblies of God, Superintendent, Southern California Network, Assemblies of God (1988–2010)

"I found Dr. Richard Varnell's book, *Let Your Church Grow,* to be a well-documented, easy-to-understand, enjoyable read. Dr. Varnell uses the teachings of Jesus Christ to illustrate a step-by-step program to grow your church's congregation. I especially enjoyed the use of Scripture quotes to validate his plan. Let me say that I learned principles from *Let Your Church Grow* that not only help pastors to grow their congregations; they also benefit one on a personal level. The Word of God is a powerful tool to spread the faith to others."

—**Ted Fisher**, Stater Brothers Employee for 41 years

"Richard Varnell may have completely revolutionized how to impact a community. I've read many books from megachurch pastors about growing one thousand+ megachurches. I can't remember a book about how to help small churches double or triple in size, even though the vast majority of churches are less than seventy-five people. Perhaps not every church is destined to be a megachurch, but every church that implements Richard's strategy will grow. If you're part of a church, you should read and implement these strategies because they are practical, doable, and will work in every church with every leader in every community every time!"

—**Craig Cunningham**, Lead Pastor, Shadow Rock Church, La Quinta, California

"Based upon my forty years of pastoral ministry, it is a blessing to be able to recommend *Let Your Church Grow* to others in pastoral ministry. Much has been written on the subject of church growth, but my friend Richard Varnell has tapped into concepts and practical applications that are within the grasp of the smaller, lower-budget congregations that do not have the needed personnel that so many strategies call for.

"It's obvious that Richard has put in much time and labor as he studied the trends and stats, and he has given several years of his life in helping local pastors to not only grow their congregations but to make their congregations the best that they can be. Job well done!

"I have found several things in Richard's book that I am seeking to employ in our congregation, and I highly recommend that pastors take the time to read this book in light of your own congregational needs. I think you will be well rewarded."

—**Bruce Dowell,** Senior Pastor. Shiloh Messianic Congregation, Crestline, California

LET YOUR CHURCH GROW

LET YOUR CHURCH GROW

RICHARD G. VARNELL

EQUIP PRESS
Colorado Springs, Colorado

LET YOUR
CHURCH
GROW

Let Your Church Grow
Copyright © 2018, Richard G. Varnell

Published by Equip Press, Colorado Springs, CO

First Edition: 2018
Let Your Church Grow / Richard G. Varnell
Paperback ISBN: 978-1-946453-33-4
eBook ISBN: 978-1-946453-32-7

CONTENTS

CHAPTER ONE

THE PROBLEM AND CURE

Approximately half of all Protestant churches in the
United States average less than seventy-five people in attendance
during their weekly morning worship services. Church growth
experts indicate that it takes about seventy-five people to support
the basic functions of a church and another fifty people to support
a pastor. The purpose of this book is to help churches reach an
average attendance of seventy-five people and to continue growing
at least until the attendance reaches a minimum of one hundred
and twenty-five people.

Churches measure how large they are in different ways. For
example, a church with a membership of five hundred may have only
one hundred people in weekly attendance, whereas another church
with fifty members may have a weekly attendance of five hundred. For
the purposes of this book, we will only measure the actual attendance
at the weekend service(s).

Over the years, I have wondered why reaching seventy-five people
in attendance was so difficult. Why do half of all Protestant churches
average less than seventy-five people? From personal experience,
I have found that reaching sixty people in attendance is the most

difficult of all goals. This book will unveil the critical components of reaching the first sixty people while also enabling church leaders to take their church to the next level of seventy-five attendees and beyond. The principles in this book are based on biblical teaching and sound business concepts. Pastors can expect their churches to grow to the goal that God has placed in their heart.

This is not a "get rich quick" scheme but rather a "growing a church the Bible way" plan. This proven plan will work 100 percent of the time. How can I give such a guarantee? Because Jesus declared, "I will build my church" (Matt. 16:18). I firmly believe that if a church is not growing, it is not functioning 100 percent as Christ intended it to function.

Most churches do not grow to over seventy-five in attendance for very simple reasons. First, pastors overestimate what they can do in the short-run and underestimate what they can do in the long-run. Second, church leaders often ignore basic Scripture-based business strategies when it comes to growing the local church.

By using the principles in this book, I will show you how to take the smallest church in attendance and bring it to at least seventy-five people. These principles work even if you are planting a church and do not have any attendees yet. They will also work if the church you are pastoring is averaging in the twenties and has been in existence for over fifty years.

I will also give you a biblical foundation for growing your church to seventy-five people. Once you understand these principles, you will more readily achieve your attendance goals. Why? Because you will understand that God is on your side and is cheering for you to make it to the first seventy-five in attendance. Second, the stories that I will give you are all personal in nature. We all learn best through our own failures and successes. Some readers might pose a basic question: "What is the big deal about getting a church to seventy-five in attendance? Anyone should be able to do that!" I agree but gathering the first seventy-five people represents a lot of hard work. If it is easy, why are half of the 344,000 American Protestant churches struggling to get there?

Many of these churches have existed for a very long time. I have been involved in churches that averaged twenty to fifty people for more than thirty years. They even had long-term pastors (more than ten-year tenures). What are the chances that these churches can change and grow to seventy-five people? Statistically speaking, they are low. If you are pastoring one of these churches, this book is designed to give you hope.

If your church has plateaued or is declining in attendance, this book is also for you. While I will give you different ideas and methods, I usually focus on how an individual pastor, without a lot of outside help, can see the church reach the goal of seventy-five people in attendance and then go beyond. While it can be done without outside help, having assistance enables you to see blind spots. It will also enable more rapid growth in your church. For instance, you could reach a three-year growth goal in one year with additional help from qualified people.

The longer you have been pastoring a church, the easier it is to overlook hindrances to your growth. Thus, having an outside consultant can provide a fresh perspective and assist you in identifying areas in need of attention. However, self-study is always the key, which can occur through reading books on church growth. Do not limit yourself to church growth materials. Study books on business growth and be a lifetime learner. You may want to learn something about calculus that shows how best to plot changes in motion, study books on marketing, or look at the newest multimedia methods. Include books on how to get along with people, conflict resolution, financial management, income taxes, and proper methods of investing. Most importantly, whatever you are learning, set aside time each day or week for study outside of your regular sermon preparation time.

As a full-time pastor, it is easy to become myopic in both behavior and outlook. This type of pastor only associates with people in his or her congregation. The church serves as a safety zone. When the pastor and his or her spouse go out to eat, they automatically invite someone from the church to join the meal. The men's breakfast only incorporates men from their own church. Likewise, staff and board meetings are composed only of people with whom they closely associate. These pastors even find it difficult to visit other churches to glean ideas because they rarely miss a Sunday morning service at their own church!

You do not need to reinvent the wheel to have a growing church. God has given church growth ideas to people since the early church. God wants us to observe, not copy, what other leaders have done. I heard about a church that was experiencing phenomenal growth. In a couple of years, they had over two thousand people in attendance, with five services on Sunday. So, even though the church met in a rented facility in a bad area of a large city, they had identified church growth principles that worked for them. This experience helped me formulate better ideas on how to reach both the churched and unchurched.

Observing what God is doing in other locations will help you be open to church growth ideas for your own church. Oftentimes, God helps you understand church growth based on your personal experience. You might be at a museum, sports game, restaurant, live performance, or any number of places when God places something in your heart to help you implement a church growth method for your church. God made a vast world, and the more you can see what God is doing in his world, the more your heart will be open to what God wants to do at your church. The apostle Paul says, quoting from the prophet Isaiah:

> No one's ever seen or heard anything like this, never so much as imagined anything quite like it—What God has arranged for those who love him. But you've seen and heard it because God by his Spirit has brought it all out into the open before you.... Who ever knows what you're thinking and planning except you yourself? The same with God—except that he not only knows what he's thinking, but he lets us in on it. (1 Cor. 2:9–12 MSG)

Because God himself is infinite, He has an infinite number of ways to help each of his churches grow. Pastors are described in Scripture with an affectionate term—shepherds (1 Peter 5:2). Not only that, they work under the direct supervision of the Chief Shepherd, who is Jesus Christ. He is even more interested in a pastor's success than the pastor is. He will load the pastor down with ideas so that he can be the best shepherd for his flock. Ultimately, when he appears again, it is pastors that he plans to reward lavishly (1 Pet. 5:4 MSG).

CHAPTER TWO

HOW I GOT INVOLVED IN CHURCH GROWTH

ALL PASTORS ARE INTERESTED IN church growth. If you grew up in church, the tendency is to pattern your leadership skills after the pastors of the churches you attended. Consequently, your church growth examples may be very limited. The first church I pastored was in a rural area. Other pastors from my denomination were at least one hundred miles away. At the age of twenty-three, I had graduated from college with a bachelor of arts in religion, and I was ready to pastor. My first church was twelve years old, and I was the thirteenth pastor! The church averaged thirty-three people and the monthly income was $375. My salary was $15 a week plus a parsonage in which to live. I wish I could tell you that the church experienced phenomenal growth. However, my church growth skills were limited to working hard and staying there five years. The growth was slow. The attendance doubled during my tenure and financial income tripled. However, my five-year tenure broke the rapid pastoral change cycle, and for the next twenty-five years, each of the pastors was full time and the church grew to two hundred people.

I pastored two other churches, one of which was a church plant. Both churches grew but, once again, not at a rapid pace. When I was fifty-three years old, I accepted a new assignment that allowed me to minister in 150 different churches over a period of eight years.

This transition to my new assignment began ten years before, when I was forty-three. I planted a church in a desert community when I was forty years old. We wanted to acquire property and build as soon as possible. Three years later, while I was praying and meditating on how to start that process, I felt the Lord speak to me about how to get started. The church at that time had about fifty people in attendance, and I had three board members—Tom, Frank, and Bob. While it was not an audible voice, the impression I had was: have Tom find the property, have Frank get it through the building approval process, and have Bob build the building. It turned out exactly that way.

God sent another friend to me, Bob, a CPA. Bob and I were both tax consultants, and Bob gave me instructions on how to structure a partnership that would first own the property, then later donate it to the church, with a possible tax advantage to the individual partners. Tom soon located the property. It was a great five-acre parcel on a major highway. The cost was $290,000. We created a five-person partnership, which purchased the property.

First, we consulted the city, and they assured us that a church could be built on the five-acre parcel. But that was not to be the case. We spent the next twenty-six months trying to get approval. They kept telling us that if we did what they requested, everything would be fine when it finally got to the architectural review committee. For many months, we made every adjustment to our plans that the planning commission suggested. However, when we got to the architectural review committee, they said this project was not at all what they wanted. We were not only dismayed but very discouraged. (Later we found out that the city had no intention of approving the project!) We decided to sell the parcel and search for a more favorable location for building a church.

A realtor told us that although the asking price for parcels near ours was more than $500,000, realistically, we could expect to sell it for $350,000. Then after paying commissions, we would end up with about $300,000—which was just slightly more than we paid. After thinking it over, Tom said to me, "Pastor, I think we should sell it ourselves." I asked Tom how much we should ask, and he said $425,000. So, I placed a small ad in the local newspaper and almost immediately we had an offer. Six months later, we had sold the land for $425,000 cash.

Later, we found out that Frank's family had a 3 1/3-acre parcel in a nearby community. We purchased that property for $150,000 and began the building approval process again. Within about a year we were building. Our attendance was still about 50 or less, so we relied on some private loans and a lot of volunteer labor. On Easter, 1995, we dedicated the building with 120 in attendance. And to make the day even more special, my first grandchild who had been born the previous Good Friday was also dedicated to the Lord.

After the dedication, the building project had quite a bit of debt, and the roadwork out front still needed to be done. Soon after, a financial miracle took place. Bruce, my son-in-law who was a CPA, had a client who made a donation by giving us stock. When we sold the stock, the amount was $175,000. One year later, that same individual needed another tax write-off. We said, "We can help!" This time the check was for $300,000. So, one year after we finished the project, we were debt free, with $100,000 in the bank for future church plants.

Another interesting thing happened two years before, in 1993. I was elected to the district executive board of the denomination that I belong to. There are about 450 churches in that district. After experiencing the benefit of stock contributions, I encouraged our board to hire someone to visit each of our churches and share the benefits of stock contributions, as well as other planned giving benefits. A committee was formed, and, eventually, a partnership was created with our national financial services group. We then needed a director. At first, I had no interest in the job. However, our District Superintendent asked me to do the job because he said I had "fire in my bones." I accepted, and for the next eight years, I visited 150 churches, helping individuals in the churches make wills or trusts. I also helped churches that needed to borrow money for their building projects.

I made mental observations regarding why some churches were growing and others were not. My first observation focused on children's ministry. Each church that focused on children's ministry was growing. They did not view children's ministry as an appendage of the church but as important to its whole operation. I think the reason for the correlation between church growth and the health of the children's program was at least two-fold. First, growth in a local church generally has to do with attracting young families with children. Second, reaching children is a theological concept. Jesus was concerned about caring for children and he placed them as a high priority in his own ministry. Parents love their children as a gift from God. In the New Testament, parents wanted Jesus to touch and bless their children. Amazingly, Jesus' own disciples objected to his care of children. I do not know whether the disciples had children, but in either case, they saw children as an interruption and not part of the main event, so Jesus corrected them. All three synoptic Gospels record the event, but this is how Mark puts it:

> The people brought children to Jesus, hoping he might touch them. The disciples shooed them off. But Jesus was irate and let them know it: "Don't push these children away. Don't ever get between them and me. These children are at the very center of life in the kingdom. Mark this: Unless you accept God's kingdom in the simplicity of a child, you'll never get in. Then, gathering the children up in his arms, he laid his hands of blessing on them. (Mark 10:13–16 MSG)

If I ever saw a vision, it had to do with a church's children ministry. A larger church, with which I was associated, was known for its great children's program. However, during a service, parents were informed that if their children arrived late, they would not be permitted to enter the program. Even though we protested the decision, the leaders allowed it to stand. I realize it would be easy to side with the children's workers who experienced the frustration of continual interruptions due to tardiness. However, in my vision I saw a single mother at home with three small children trying to get ready for church—a shoe had been lost, something spilled, and she had misplaced her car keys. When she tried to check the children into church, they were denied. Then, I saw Jesus weeping, standing at the gate and saying, "I will take the children."

Scripture talks about carrying God's message to succeeding generations. King David longed to proclaim God's Word to those who would follow him. Part of the *imago Dei* (the image of God) in each person desires to share with the younger generation what God has deposited into his or her life. The part of us that is godlike causes us to become parents, teachers, and mentors. When we follow the Great Commission, we lead people to Christ and teach them how to be followers of Christ. The Scripture encourages us to leave an inheritance to the next generation. David says, "Now that I am old and gray, do not abandon me, O God. Let me proclaim your power to this new generation, your mighty miracles to all who come after me" (Ps. 71:18 NLT).

My second observation was that churches were not implementing normal business practices in the operations of the church. For instance, of the 150 churches I visited, only two acknowledged my attendance or the gift that I made in the offering. Each time I visited a church, I would place a gift, by way of a check, in the offering. The check had my name, date, and address. I knew the church bookkeepers would know that I was a first-time giver because they would have to record my gift as a new giver. One of the two churches that did contact me was a larger church. In essence, the letter thanked me for the gift as a first-time giver and, in a nice way, indicated this may not have been my first time to attend the church (See Appendix N).

Different things indicated that most churches were not taking advantage of the information they received from guests and did not implement available modern technologies. For instance, I conducted a survey in which I called one hundred churches during normal business hours and asked one question: "What time is your Sunday morning service?" Fifty percent of the churches either did not answer their phone or answered with some type of phone answering device. Of the fifty churches that did answer, only one followed up with any additional information or tried to find out anything about me. They did not ask if I needed help with directions or try to engage me in any type of conversation to draw me in to their church.

While half the churches did answer their phones during business hours, almost none answered their phones during a critical period. I discovered that most phone calls from first-time guests are not made during normal business hours, but rather between Saturday afternoon and service time on Sunday morning. Even though many people find churches on the internet, some people still use the phone to confirm the online information, acquire exact driving directions, or ask questions not readily available on the church website. One can easily correct this problem by forwarding the church phone to the cell phone of a "live" person after office hours and on weekends. Another solution is to contract with an answering service which, for a reasonable fee, will answer the church phone when no one is in the office.

Third, I was amazed at the number of churches that still did not have a website. For the churches that did have a website, in many cases, it was difficult to find. On the other hand, many churches that had a website did not keep the information updated. If a church cannot update their website on a weekly basis, it is better to provide a more generic website that does not require regular updates.

Fourth, I observed that most churches did not have a good program for tracking first, second, and third-time guests. Consequently, I began to put together a mental overview of what such a program would include. After explaining my ideas to a fellow pastor, he asked me if I had ever written these concepts down, to which I responded, "No, but I would be glad to do so!" Six months later, I talked with this pastor again. He said, "Do you remember those church ideas you shared with me? Well, I put them into practice and my church has grown by 50 percent—from fifty to seventy-five people. This got my attention, and I began my pilgrimage into church growth.

CHAPTER THREE

EMPOWERMENT FOR THE CHURCH

IN MY EARLY THIRTIES, I completed my master's degree in biblical studies from a seminary. After completing that degree, I pursued a bachelor of arts equivalent in business administration from a secular university. After twenty-five years of being out of school, my seminary contacted me and encouraged me to participate in a new fast track program to earn a doctor of ministry degree. I later discovered that it was not a fast track for me. For the next seven years, I worked hard to complete the program and, finally, at age sixty-eight, I received my degree. The core courses were great. We would read two thousand pages prior to the class, write some reports, then gather on campus for one week, three times a year. After completing the one-week module, I would have sixty days to submit a paper. Since there were usually only twelve to fifteen students in a class, I enjoyed interacting with my professors and fellow students.

After being in the program for a while, I needed to select a subject for my project, which is similar to a dissertation in that it incorporated a large amount of research and writing. The doctoral team rejected my first project idea because they felt that it did not solve a problem. I wanted to do research on the "Influence of One Church." The church in which I grew up started in 1925 and closed in 1989. My intent was to do research on people who attended the church during that period to see how it had affected their lives. I did some research and the results were amazing. However, that was not to be my project.

Due to the leadership position I held with the group of churches to which I belong, my primary focus was on church growth. After doing preliminary research, I decided to title my project "Stimulating Church Growth Through Scripturally Based Business Strategies: Targeting Churches Plateaued or Declining in Attendance."

Initially, I focused on determining whether the concept of church growth was a biblical concept. If not, I would not have a project. However, as I conducted further biblical studies on church growth, I became more convinced that it was an integral part of Bible doctrine. My research convinced me that much of Bible doctrine and, in particular, church growth, was found in the first chapter of the Bible—Genesis 1. I soon realized that some of my colleagues could interpret my church growth ideas as simply gimmicks. The concepts always worked, but some people saw the principles as a worldly attempt to get people to attend church and to increase church attendance. Nevertheless, my research repeatedly confirmed that God wants his church to grow and that he has provided methods to make that happen. I also learned that church growth is hard work that requires relentless passion and steady consistency. Almost all church growth is gradual, with some exceptions like the Day of Pentecost or historically recorded revivals where the church, for a time, grew rapidly. However, most revivals last approximately three years and then it is back to hard work!

The most important words about church growth in the New Testament came from Jesus when he said, "I will build my church" (Matt. 16:18 NIV). When Jesus spoke those words, he also gave believers wisdom, power, and the Holy Spirit to help them accomplish the task. Jesus taught his followers to pray, "Your will be done on earth as it is in heaven" (v. 10). As church leaders and believers follow him, God will answer that prayer and individual churches will reach their maximum potential.

If a church has not flourished over a long time, one can assume that it has not appropriated all the provisions for church health that Christ has made available. Ultimately, this reiterates the basic assumption that every church can grow to become all that Christ desires. This, however, requires church leaders and members to explicitly listen to and apply the principles provided by the church founder—Jesus Christ! Without a doubt, Jesus wants each local church to grow and be healthy—even more so than the pastor. In other words, the founder and church leaders have the same goal.

Successful church growth requires an understanding of the biblical concept of the image of God, often referred to as the *imago Dei*. In my opinion, the most important verses in the Old Testament about church growth are Genesis 1:26–28:

> Then God said, "Let us make man in our image, in our likeness, and let them rule over the fish of the sea and the birds of the air, over the livestock, over all the earth, and over all the creatures that move along the ground." So God created man in his own image, in

the image of God he created him; male and female
he created them. God blessed them and said to them,
"Be fruitful and increase in number; fill the earth and
subdue it. Rule over the fish of the sea, and the birds
of the air and over every living creature that moves on
the ground."

Biblical teaching indicates that God has always existed, so the
logical question arises: "Why did God create humankind?" God
already had everything. He spoke billions of universes into existence.
He made the earth habitable with vegetation and animals who would
always obey him. It appears that he had already had trouble with
angels. Even after creating everything, something was still lacking
in God's eternal plan. Humankind seems to be God's last creative
act and his crowning glory. When God created people, he had
great eternal hopes. Gilbert Bilezikian says it well: "God could not
reproduce himself and create another God since he is absolute and,
therefore, unique. But God did the next best thing. He created beings
in his image. This was the closest he could get to giving of himself
without compromising his own divine nature."

Because of sin, Jesus, the second person of the Trinity, came
to earth to bring us back to God so that God's eternal plan could
continue. God expresses his passionate love for us in John 3:16 (NIV):
"For God so loved the world that he gave his one and only Son, that
whoever believes in him shall not perish but have eternal life."

Humankind's desire to be in community stems from being
created in the nature of a triune God. Bilezikian describes the yearning
people feel because of sin: "Buried deep within every human soul
throbs a muted pain that never goes away. It is a lifelong yearning

for that one love that will never be found. Our mourning is for the closeness that was ours by right of creation. Our grief is for the gift lost in the turmoil of rebellion." Scripture establishes the community of the Godhead—Father, Son, and Holy Spirit. What humanity lost in rebellion can only be restored through a relationship with Christ and his church. God never intended for people to be alone, and the desire to be in relationship with one another reflects the communal aspect of being created in the image of God.

God chose to replicate himself through humankind. Jesus made a unique request: "That all of them be one, Father, just as you are in me and I am you" (John 17:21 NIV). Three times in John 17, Jesus requests that his followers be one with God like Christ is one with the Father. God desires that humanity be in community with him, just as the Father, Son, and Holy Spirit are in community with each other. This applies equally to the church and individual Christ-followers, as Scriptures instruct believers to be holy just as God is holy (Lev. 20:7; 1 Pet. 1:15–16).

1. Empowerment through Community

When God's people are in community with the triune God, as he intended, they can accomplish the things he has empowered them to do through his Word. Jesus sent his disciples out into the world to proclaim God's kingdom, heal the sick, raise the dead, and drive out demons. Jesus affirms the closeness of community by saying: "Freely you have received, freely give" (Matt. 10:8 NIV). Christ not only brings believers into community with the triune God so they can experience wonderful fellowship through prayer and meditation but also to accomplish his will on earth as it is in heaven. God's intent is to bring believers together so they can grow. Mike Clarensau observes: "A growing church isn't a bad thing. In fact, that's the plan Jesus had when he launched the Great Commission. The book of Acts tells of no spiritual islands, where small gatherings of saints simply existed in spiritual isolation."

2. Community in the Life of Christ

Upon beginning his public ministry, Jesus intently focused on creating a community of believers who would not only follow in his footsteps while he lived on earth but also to establish a self-perpetuating community for all eternity. He empowered his disciples for the present and also the future, when he will inaugurate a new millennial community. Jesus not only spoke about community, he established community.

Jesus illustrated the importance of community by how he used his time. Recognizing the importance of perpetuating the gospel until the end of the ages, Jesus primarily focused attention on his disciples. He took advantage of teaching them heavenly concepts through parables. If they did not understand the parables, he privately explained their meanings. Multiple times, Christ revealed to his disciples the plan for his death, burial, and resurrection. Julie A. Gorman rightly asserts: "The Gospels show truth and life as seen through the eyes of the community in which he invested his life and energy. Who he was is revealed to them. How he taught and lived is experienced by them."

Jesus did not minimize the individual characteristics of his disciples but trained them to work together because he realized the importance of community among the Twelve. When the Twelve worked together as a group, the whole was greater than the sum of each working individually. This became especially evident following the death of Jesus as the disciples met and rehearsed the loneliness they felt—both individually and as a group. After Jesus' resurrection, the disciples stayed together as a group. Jesus even appeared to them as a group and continued to instruct them (Mark 16:9-18; Luke 24:36–49, John 20:19–29; 1 Cor. 15:5–8). After the departure of Judas, Scripture refers to the "eleven disciples."

Jesus gave the "Great Commission" to the eleven remaining disciples. After Jesus' ascension to heaven, the angels address the eleven as "Men of Galilee" (Acts 1:11). The importance of the group was so significant that a few days after the ascension of Jesus, a study of the Old Testament Scriptures determined that someone must be appointed to take the place of Judas (Acts 1:21–26). Scripture indicates, "Without guidance, a people will fall, but there is victory with many counselors" (Prov. 11:14 CEB). Solomon bemoans the folly of being alone: "How miserable are those who fall and don't have a companion to help them up" (Eccl. 4:10 CEB)! God brings people into community for fellowship and effective evangelism.

3. The Value of Community

Living in community is a biblical concept rooted deeply in the *imago Dei*. God never intended for people to take living in community lightly. For the early church, community was not optional but rather a command that would make it possible to follow in the footsteps of Christ. Jesus held a high view of community, so much so that he promised to be present in a unique way when the church gathered in his name:

> "Take this most seriously: A yes on earth is yes in heaven; a no on earth is no in heaven. What you say to one another is eternal. I mean this. When two

of you get together on anything at all on earth and make a prayer of it, my Father in heaven goes into action. And when two or three of you are together because of me, you can be sure that I'll be there." (Matt. 18:18–20 MSG)

While community is God's plan for his people, it does not happen automatically. Searching to be part of a God-given community is worth the effort, but simply attending a church does not suddenly bring a person into a community. Depending on the size of the church, a person may need to seek intentional avenues that lead to inclusion in the community. A major part of this project is helping churches develop community for everyone who walks through the door. A church must purposefully develop a community plan for those who already attend the local assembly and cultivate a plan to include first-time guests and those who are unchurched.

One of the purposes of the church is to reach, through evangelism, those who have not yet decided to follow Christ as their personal Savior. As the church seeks to reach the unchurched with the gospel of Jesus Christ, God will equip church leaders with creative ideas that will help them successfully reach and disciple people in their community. Churches that vigorously pursue available tools for evangelism will quickly learn that the Eternal One himself will provide the necessary assistance along the way.

The earliest Christians understood that by following the teachings of Jesus they formed a new type of all-encompassing community. This was to be a radically inclusive group. Male and female, rich and poor, master and slave were all brought together to form the church. No true follower of Jesus, despite his or her background or ethnicity, was to be excluded. How they treated each other determined their own inclusion in this new group. Jesus stated it this way, "So now I am giving you a new commandment: Love each other. Just as I have loved you, you should love each other. Your love for one another will prove to the world that you are my disciples" (John 13:34–35 NLT).

A community that serves God does not appear overnight but rather develops when God's people understand that by working together, they can more effectively accomplish his will than they can alone. As people created in the image of God, believers participate in a community inspired and directed by God himself. In essence, living in community with other believers reflects the community demonstrated within the Godhead. Community, as established by God when he created humankind in his own image, will endure for both time and eternity. This new community actually goes to heaven together no matter where in history an individual joined the community of Christ, as seen in 1 Thessalonians 4:16–17:

> For the Lord himself will come down from heaven, with a loud command, with the voice of the archangel and with the trumpet call of God, and the dead in Christ will rise first. After that, we who are still alive and are left will be caught up together with them in the clouds to meet the Lord in the air. And so we will be with the Lord forever. (NIV)

4. Growth—God's Plan

All healthy children grow. From birth onward, parents can see the growth of their children. In fact, they expect their child to grow; if the child does not grow, the parents become concerned. Only by measuring growth periodically can one know the exact amount of growth. Some years a child grows more than other years, but growth is a normal part of life.

I enjoyed measuring the growth of both my children and grandchildren. You may relate to the routine. I would get a book, a pencil, measuring tape, and the child, and we would march to the wall on the other side of the door or in the garage. Once the proper mark was made, we would compare it to the last mark—usually a year ago. One time, I waited a year and a half to measure my grandchildren and they had grown between five and seven inches each. We celebrated their growth.

God planned for humankind to grow. After God created Adam and Eve, he said, "Be fruitful and increase in number; fill the earth" (Gen. 1:28 NIV). After the flood, God repeated these same words to Noah and his three sons as they left the ark. The world population has continued to grow and now stands at more than 7 billion. Scholars estimate that 108 billion people have lived on earth. Today's population is 6 percent of the number who have ever lived.

The Bible illustrates the importance of keeping numerical track of humankind's activities. God used numbers, from Genesis to Revelation, to help track his dealings and interactions with people and his creation. Scripture uses numbers to show both the passage of time and to indicate growth. In fact, Scripture begins with an account of the seven days of creation and ends with the size of the New Jerusalem. God knows when a sparrow falls to the ground, and he numbers the hairs on each person's head. One book of the Bible is even named Numbers!

One must periodically measure growth to determine the amount of change over a given period. Churches that do not keep track of growth cannot know where they should be in God's plan. Clarensau identifies the importance of measuring church growth: "So how is your church doing at assimilating its guests? Churches need times of assessment, too. A church's ability to retain its guests reveals much about its effectiveness in reaching people."

When recording growth, one must use the numbers accurately. An old adage says, "Figures don't lie, but liars do figure." Measuring growth requires accuracy and an unbiased opinion. The richest and most generous person in American history was John D. Rockefeller. Ron Chernow describes Rockefeller's emphasis on record keeping: "For Rockefeller, ledgers were sacred books that guided decisions and saved one from fallible emotion. They gauged performances, exposed fraud, and ferreted out hidden inefficiencies. In an imprecise world, they rooted things in a solid empirical reality." Rockefeller, when talking about his rivals, said: "Many of the brightest kept their books in such a way that they did not actually know when they were making money on a certain operation and when they were losing." Local church growth, in like manner, must include accurate assessments so we will know when we are gaining people or losing them.

Church leaders must use the accumulation of data to analyze the church's growth cycle and project future plans. A church should appropriately celebrate its growth, much like what occurred after Peter's sermon on the Day of Pentecost when three thousand people were added to their number. How did they celebrate? In both the Old and New Testaments, God commanded his people to have celebrations to remind them of his love and care. McIntosh makes the following observation: "Israel was to practice these celebrations even when they were in difficult situations. As you work to revitalize your church, keep the same idea in mind. Whenever you have the smallest of triumphs, celebrate them." Ultimately, the church must hold itself accountable for and celebrate its own growth.

CHAPTER FOUR

HELP!

THIS CHAPTER WILL DISCUSS four churches where I served as a church growth consultant. To be included in the project, the attendance of the church must have an average of fewer than two hundred people in weekly attendance and have demonstrated a plateau or decline in attendance over the past three years. The purpose was to test the church growth principles I had developed in the most challenging circumstances and to find out if these principles would work everywhere—under all situations. Church statistics reveal an abundance of churches that fall into these categories!

In America, there are 344,000 Protestant churches. Eighty-four percent have less than two hundred people in weekly attendance while 60 percent of those churches are either plateaued or declining. Essentially, 173,000 churches in America fall into this category! Another interesting statistic is that half of the churches in America average less than seventy-five individuals in weekly attendance. When you combine that information with the fact that 3,000 to 4,000 churches in America close each year, one can easily ascertain that churches need help. Rainer states that 100,000 churches in America are showing signs of decline toward death. However, the Scriptures clearly indicate that the harvest is large and the laborers are few (Matt. 8:37; Luke 10:2).

Churches with an average attendance of seventy-five people or fewer and an attendance plateau or decline for the past three years usually demonstrate common characteristics. First, these types of churches will most likely close their doors in the next five to ten years. Second, churches in that category probably cannot reverse the trend without outside help. Obviously, one person alone cannot personally help all 100,000 churches in need of assistance. Therefore, together, we must build helpers to assist these churches.

Third, only some declining and plateaued churches really want help. Helping a church that does not really want to change is an effort in futility. However, I have yet to find a church that says, "We don't want to grow." The conversation usually goes like this: "I do not know why we are not growing; we are a very friendly church." The statement was true; however, they are only friendly to each other because they ignore all first-time guests.

Change, for many people and most churches, is not easy. For most plateaued or declining churches, a change in the church culture must take place. By culture, I mean the way individuals in the church naturally view and treat people unlike themselves—whether we're talking about those who currently attend the church or those who come for the first time. We must constantly remind ourselves that being a follower of Christ causes Christians to love each other, thus declaring our love for Christ. Is it possible for long-standing members of a church to act poorly toward each other and in front of other church attendees? I recently experienced a shouting match during the morning worship time over who was allowed in the nursery. Division in the church is nothing new! Even the apostle Paul states that Alexander, the metalworker, had done him much harm (2 Tim. 4:14).

I was once part of a committee that supervised smaller churches. The committee had the responsibility for the health of the smaller churches and was charged with recommending whether the pastor should stay another term. The committee met with the pastor of a declining church to help him see the importance of church growth. He refuted every suggestion with an obstacle for why it would not work. After a long discussion and little progress, the pastor stated that unless the Lord told him to leave the church, he would not—even if the attendance went to zero.

Yes, change is hard, and it takes hard work to change. Since so many churches need help, we must limit our help to churches that are willing to make the necessary changes in their culture to produce a church that is Christ-honoring. Although churches of all sizes may need cultural adjustments, I have purposed to focus my efforts on churches I feel called to help. A founding pastor of a larger church felt that after fifteen years, some things in the culture of the church needed to change. Implementing the change was painful, and two hundred people left the church. However, now the church has 1,400 people and they are planting another church.

When consulting with churches or giving seminars on church growth, I find that many pastors are fearful about making the necessary changes for their church to grow. When implementing cultural changes in a church, one must use quality leadership skills. Whether your church is averaging twenty, two hundred, or two thousand, you need to be at your God-given best to make changes in the culture of the church you pastor. Happily, this can be done without sinking the ship!

The most difficult case I heard about was of a new pastor coming to a historic church. The church had been in existence for three hundred years, it had been in decline for many years, and the retiring pastor of thirty years was both staying in the community and in the church. The new pastor decided to honor the past while simultaneously casting a vision for the future. Over the next nine months, the pastor and his wife dedicated three nights a week to invite thirty attendees to their home for food and fellowship. What a commitment, but it worked! The attendance decline reversed, and the church went on to establish itself in a new way.

The Bible tells us that if we need wisdom, God will grant our request for his help. No situation is too difficult for an eternal, all-knowing, and all-powerful God. The Scripture asks a critical question: "If God is for us who can be against us?" (Rom. 8:31). Since it is Christ's plan for his church to continue to grow, he gives inquiring hearts the answers to see the local church flourish.

5. The Basis of the Project

The project entailed a specific process, whereby the church could track first-time guests and follow-up with guests as well as regular attendees. It also involved in helping the church establish a phone answering service so a live person would answer the phone 24/7. To provide quality treatment of first-time guests, we increased the number of ushers by three or four-fold. Also, we encouraged the church to designate special parking for first-time guests.

6. Tracking First-Time Guests and Regular Attendees

To track first-time guests and regular attendees, the church introduced the use of the "Getting to Know You… (a little better) Card" (see Appendix D). Each family present during the Sunday morning worship service filled out the card. The pastor set the example by completing the card as well. Musicians played softly in the background while people completed the card and ushers collected them. The church repeated this process for the next two Sundays to include individuals not present the previous Sundays.

The following week, the church input the information collected from the "Getting to Know You Cards" into an electronic spreadsheet. Based on the list, the church prepared printed nametags for each person and distributed them to attendees the following Sunday. Depending on how well the program was introduced to the congregation, there was generally a 2 percent resistance rate to wearing the nametags. Most resistance was overcome by further explanation.

Starting with the second Sunday service and every Sunday afterwards, the pastor allotted time for everyone to finish the Getting to Know You Card. This weekly exercise played an essential role in the program. The pastor completed his card while the congregants filled in their cards and ushers collected the cards with the offering. Use of the Getting to Know You Card provides a means of communication suitable for both regular attendees and guests. Most high assimilation churches use a similar card. One of the many advantages of doing this together as a congregation is that guests are not singled out. They simply do what everyone else is doing.

Each week, the church staff tallied the cards and recorded the attendance in an electronic spreadsheet. To provide accurate attendance information for each Sunday service, staff also tapped into other records. For instance, the nametags that were not picked up indicate the people who were absent. Children's attendance was tallied by checking the sign-in records from the age appropriate ministries. Giving records also helped determine the attendance of all givers.

7. Establishing a Follow-Up Plan

Each Monday, the church compiled the data collected during the previous Sunday morning service. If a regular attendee was absent one time but a staff member knew why, no follow-up was needed. However, if a regular attendee was absent and no one knew why, the person was sent a "Missing in Action" Letter (MIA Letter) (See Appendix F). If the regular attendee had been absent two or more Sundays, the church personally contacted the person with a phone call or a visit.

When a person gave an offering for the first time, it triggered another follow-up system. First, the church would send the first-time giver a "Thank You Letter" (See Appendix G). Second, the first-time giver received three additional contacts that week: (1) an email designed to arrive on Monday between 3 and 4 p.m., (2) a phone call, and (3) a thirty-second visit to his or her home with a small gift (by Friday afternoon). Each contact should extend an invitation for the person to attend the coming Sunday worship service.

First-, second-, and third-time guests should receive a letter from the church (see Appendix H, I, and J). If the guest made a contribution, the letter should express appreciation for the contribution (see Appendix G and K). Once the guest had attended the church three times, the pastor or a staff member contacted the guest and arranged for a time to meet. The purpose of the meeting was to assimilate the guest into the local church. If a first-time guest did not return for a month, the church sent him or her an email or letter indicating that the church was still thinking about them (see Appendix M).

8. Implementing an Answering Service

A final component of the project included the establishment of an answering service to cover the church phone when the office was closed. The answering service provided basic information such as service times and church address. In addition, the answering service forwarded emergency calls to the proper staff person. All project participants received this service.

9. Implementing the Project

Church A

When I met the pastor of Church A, he had been senior pastor for just eight months but had been on staff at the church for the previous five years. The church attendance had basically plateaued, with a slight decline in the past several years. The church is located in a larger city, with a good location and enough facilities to grow to more than five hundred. The church had been in existence for at least seventy-five years and had reached its highest attendance in the 1960s. Initially, the pastor and I met for three hours, and I discerned that he wanted his church to grow.

We started the registration part of the project on a Sunday soon after we met. It went very well, and the first Sunday we gave nametags to each person was a success. The project lasted for five months. I met with the pastor and staff weekly in addition to being present at several of the Sunday morning services.

The pastor and staff worked hard each week to implement the program. First-time guests were greeted well each Sunday. Each week, the staff sent letters to first-, second-, or third-time guests to let them know their attendance was appreciated. The last month of the program was July and the average attendance was 178. The average attendance for July for the three previous years was 145, which represented a 23 percent increase in attendance.

Church B

Church B was the most challenging church in my project. This neighborhood church, in a city of 50,000, is located on a busy street, has adequate parking, and has educational buildings for their eighty-seat sanctuary. The pastor had been there six years and worked another full-time job. The church had an average attendance in the thirties and had been in decline for several years. The church was in the church growth program for twelve weeks. Even though the pastor worked full-time outside the church, he did not even have secretarial help. Consequently, my team printed the weekly nametags, kept attendance records, and mailed the follow-up letter to the guests. Someone from my team attended most Sunday services to help implement the program.

The program never quite took hold. However, it did create some enthusiasm and there was some growth. The previous year had seen a sharp decrease in attendance, with the last month of the year averaging twenty-eight. The average attendance for the first four weeks of the program was thirty-two people; average attendance for the last four weeks was forty-one people, an increase of 28 percent. However, enthusiasm for the program decreased toward the end and led to the discontinuance of the program.

Church C

Church C is located in a rural town of about 20,000 and is located on the corner of two busy streets and near some businesses.

The sanctuary seats about 150 people, but their parking area does not provide adequate space for their sanctuary capacity. In addition, they have limited educational buildings. The current pastor has served the church for ten years in which time the church reached its fifty-year record of 150 people. The church was in the program for seven months, was well-organized, and meticulously followed the program. The project gave impetus to the church attendance, producing an average attendance of 149 people, an 11 percent increase for the same period over the previous year.

Church D

Church D, located in a rural area about one mile from the main highway, averaged between thirty and forty people each week for the past forty years. The sanctuary seats approximately one hundred people and there is enough parking, but the parking lot is not paved. However, they lack educational rooms, and their four-thousand-square-foot facility does not have air conditioning, which poses a problem in a desert climate. The average attendance for July of the current year was twenty-eight. The church had been in a non-growth period in attendance, but recent months indicate a decline. We implemented the project in August even though they did not have a permanent pastor. They were part of the project for twelve weeks, and I served as interim pastor for that period.

The church quickly responded to the program with the following average attendances: August was thirty-one; September forty-two, and the first three weeks in October when the program concluded was fifty-two. Church D experienced a growth of 86 percent between July to late October.

10. Results of the Project

General Observations

Unfortunately, none of the four churches followed the program 100 percent. The church with the best level of participation adopted about half of the program's processes. The level to which the church adopted the program's processes usually depended on the senior pastor's involvement. As a result of implementing this project, I learned that adopting the program for church growth also required the church to change its culture and attitudes toward first-time guests.

All four of the participating churches had a weak greeter and usher staff. Some first-time guests at the two largest churches (Church A and C) occasionally arrived at the morning worship service more than one hour late, and no one was available to greet them. At first, none of the four churches had greeters available to welcome first-time guests after the first fifteen minutes of the morning worship. At the start of the program, none of the churches provided assistance to first-time guests as they made their way from the parking lot to the church building. Initially, none of the churches used a communication card or had a plan for following up with first-, second-, and third-time guests. At the beginning of the project, none of the churches took attendance; therefore, they had no means by which to know which regular attendees were absent.

The use of nametags for morning worship service attendees had three unexpected results. First, during the "Friendship Time," there was much more excitement and conversation with both the regular attendees and the first-time guests. No matter how small the church is, an individual usually does not know everyone attending the church. Some people who consider the church their home church may come infrequently, and first-, second-, and third-time guests have yet to meet most of the people attending the morning worship service. With the nametags, people could easily address one another by name, which resulted in greater participation during that part of the service.

Second, the attendance began to increase even though other parts of the program had not yet been implemented. When a church becomes intentional about church growth, regular attendees become more interested in inviting their friends to attend church. Third, since all regular attendees had pre-printed nametags available, unused tags identified absentees. The church could use this information to help them connect with regular attendees who had been absent.

11. Hope for Pastors of Struggling Churches

This project should prove helpful on several levels. First, it will provide hope to pastors of either plateaued or declining churches. They will be able to see that the implementation of business strategies can increase both attendance and finances.

Second, leaders will learn how to assimilate both regular and new attendees into the local church. They will learn that by systematically placing people into ministry opportunities, people will enjoy a sense of fulfillment as they work together for common causes.

Third, pastors will learn methods to implement stewardship principles in church growth. In turn, this will help the church meet its financial needs and experience growth in spiritual maturity among attendees, which generates collective enthusiasm.

Fourth, because the church will have a plan for assimilation, new believers will quickly be integrated into the life and ministry of the church. New believers will be encouraged to join discipleship programs for spiritual growth.

Fifth, once churches begin to grow through the application of business strategies, a ripple effect will begin to occur. The churches will begin to look for other ways ministries could create growth. With the increased attendance, financial giving will increase, thereby enabling the church to develop its ministry to children and youth. They might begin giving more toward local and global missions, which will result in further spiritual, financial, and numerical growth. This positive snowball effect will bring both growth and enthusiasm to the local church.

Last, implementing the basic business principles presented in this project will reduce the decline in attendance among American churches. As pastors experience growth first-hand, they will share their experiences with other pastors, thereby creating a cycle of continual church growth among previously plateaued or declining churches. Ultimately, implementation of this project could help avoid the unnecessary closure of American churches and break the cycle of declining or plateauing churches among America's churches. God desires to expand his kingdom through the church; therefore, he has made abundant provisions for each church to grow at his determined rate.

CHAPTER FIVE

AT ATTENTION

12. Passion

MOST OF US IN ministry have learned that when God gives us a passion for something, it is for a reason. Some of us, like Moses, Gideon, or many other Bible figures, might be telling God why we are not qualified to do a certain job. At other times, it becomes like fire in our bones and contentment comes only as we begin, by faith, to do what God is calling us to do.

As I worked on this project, my passion for church growth intensified. The big question was whether I had developed a principle for church growth. A principle is a rule or law that should work in every situation with few, if any, exceptions. For instance, in the business world, some leaders adopt the principle that the customer is *always* right. If you believe that principle, you look for the worst possible customer and apply your principle to that person. Most people in the business world realize that the customer may be wrong, but regardless, you must treat the customers as if they are correct. If your business is focused on profit, some people feel that the money earned from a difficult customer is the same as that earned from a pleasant customer.

In the religious world, we understand that Jesus Christ himself created the church universal. However, calling your organization a church does not necessarily make it a church, any more than calling yourself a doctor makes you a doctor. I guess it is possible for a church to cease being a church if it no longer recognizes Christ as its head. So, putting aside some irregularities, let's make the statement that every church can grow.

Closing churches is a serious problem. Some researchers suggest that 100,000 churches are on their way to closing. These statistics are difficult to ascertain because hundreds of church groups exist, along with many churches that are independent of a parent organization. It is estimated that 344,000 Protestant churches exist in America and approximately 3,000 to 4,000 churches close each year, which is about 1 percent. I measured one growing denomination and their closure rate was less than 2 percent. Keep in mind that when we read the parable of the lost sheep, Jesus is not content with a 1 percent attrition rate. However big or small the problem may be, we in the church world would like to keep it to a minimum. Pastors and parishioners alike grieve at the closure of a church—whether the church you pastored or the church you used to attend. It definitely does not involve celebration.

Some people try to view the closing of a local church intellectually. They study the life cycle of the church and conclude that church closures are inevitable and even expected. I believe the primary reason for allowing a church to close is when it stops being a church in the biblical sense and has morphed into a social club or another type of organization. When people enter a local church, they should see a group of people endeavoring to follow Christ to the best of their abilities.

There are times when a local church must close or relocate. For instance, a church might need to close because people no longer attend and it is just an empty building. Or perhaps the debt could not be paid or the deferred maintenance makes it impossible to continue. On other occasions, the church may be renting or leasing a building, and they lose their lease. Aside from some extraordinary reasons, we want to focus on each church being able to grow.

13. An Example

I finally had the opportunity to pastor a church that would put all my church growth principles to the test. I was only supposed to be there for a short period but ended up staying a year and a half. I had known about the church for several years and had served as an outside board member for a season. This rural church had been in existence for sixty years, but the attendance was in the twenties and declining, and the church had a large amount of deferred maintenance in their property. The attendance had been on a slow decline for many years. However, I saw potential for this underutilized church because it was located near a large military base. Unfortunately, only one family from the base was attending the church.

Assessment

When revitalizing a local church, one must conduct a critical analytic assessment of the situation. First, one must assess the ultimate potential for church attendance without relocating. Because it takes approximately 125 people to support a building and a pastor, you should seriously consider whether to start the process if you do not see the potential for growth. Once the church achieves an attendance of 125 people and has no way to expand at that location, the church may be large enough to think about relocating.

The first issue to assess is the physical barriers to church growth. In my situation, the church had enough buildings for growth (5,100 square feet). However, the church faced three major challenges. First, the children's building (2,700 square feet) was sixty years old and was uninhabitable. Most parents would not want to allow their children in the building. Second, none of the church buildings had air conditioning, and the church was located in the desert. Third, the church only had six paved parking spots, which made it difficult to get into the buildings. To complicate the situation further, I was only available one day per week and on the weekends.

To address these physical challenges, I put together a small team. It included my friend David, who lived in the area and had served with me on another board. David had been in the construction field most of his adult life and had a great heart for ministry. My wife, Joy, and I met David and his wife, Patti, for a meal. I explained to David the challenges, and he was in! We met with the church board, which consisted of two individuals from the church and one outside board member from another church.

David drew up plans for remodeling the children's building. To make the building useable, we had to tear everything down to the studs, put in new plumbing and electrical, new handicap restrooms, new kitchen, and air conditioning. The cost would be about $90,000. Our goal was to do it in fifty-two days, like the remodeling of the temple. After completing the children's building, we planned to remodel the worship center with new carpet, paint, chairs, and air conditioning. The last project would focus on paving the parking lot. The work on the children's building took ninety days while the remodel on the worship center took two months. The parking lot was finished nine months after the work was initiated. In the end, the remodel cost a total of $200,000 and a lot of donated labor.

The next person to join my team was Chris, a talented brother who had previously served as a senior pastor and as an executive pastor. As executive pastor, he had helped his previous church grow from 125 people to 1,400 people. As a highly skilled administrator and person gifted in business programs, Chris worked with me at the church at least one day a week, training some church members and doing much of the work himself.

Blessing Others

Something unusual happened the first Sunday I spoke at the church, which was in the month of January. A Samoan church group had previously contacted me about renting our facilities on Sunday afternoons. Upon consulting the previous pastor, I learned that a previous group that rented the facility failed to pay the rent. However, that January morning, the Samoan church leaders from one hundred miles away, along with the pastor of their local church, walked in during Sunday School hour. We quickly pulled together the board and held a meeting. I mentioned the previous problem and the Samoan group leader said he would guarantee the rent. One of our board members said, "We're brothers. Let's give it a try." It was one of our best decisions ever. The Samoan church joined us and is still meeting there today. They became great workers on each of our remodeling projects and occasionally joined our morning worship services, providing music the way Samoans do so well.

Challenges

One of my first goals was to attract people from the military base. This required focusing on three groups: (1) single military recruits with an average age of 19; (2) young married couples with one child, with an average age of 18–23; and (3) career military and officers, with an average age of 30. To meet the needs of these people, we changed three basic things: the music, the nursery, and the children's program. At first, no children regularly attended the services. The children that did attend were usually first-time guests. However, I hired a lady from the military base to work in the nursery with children ages 0–3. She worked for six months, with no children in that age bracket attending the services, but we were prepared when they did come. We changed our music program by using instruments rather than recorded music. My wife, Joy, and the one military wife started the children's program.

As I pulled into the parking lot that first Sunday, one of the women greeted me, but she was crying. See wanted me to take over her duties. Every Sunday was both a challenge and an opportunity. Some people had wanted to quit, but God told them to stay. One couple was unhappy with the duties that the previous pastor had given them, which resulted in another crying session and, eventually, they left the church. Overall, most of the people who remained accepted the changes as graciously as possible.

During the remodel of the children's building, all events shifted to the worship center. The attendance on my first Sunday was twenty-six and the lowest it reached was the next month at nineteen. The attendance stayed relatively low until September, when the attendance was fifty people on a regular Sunday.

Welcome Cards

We immediately started the guest retention program. We used welcome cards to record each person's contact information and each week we provided name tags. At my request, Daniel and Victoria, the young military couple, served as greeters. Subsequently, Victoria served in our children's program and worked in the church office during the week. Eventually, she became the children's program director. We also immediately began membership classes. Initially, the attendance progress was slow, but there was a growing sense of excitement each week. As soon as the children's building was completed, we started a monthly lunch following the morning worship service.

Almost all churches need either a cultural change or adjustment. The reason most churches are not growing is they have not learned how to convert a first-time guest into a second-time attendee. Each week, we would record the attendance in an electronic spreadsheet. We compared our ushers' count with the spreadsheet to ensure that we did not miss anyone. We also used our giving record, along with the sign-in sheets from the nursery and children's church, to make the count as accurate as possible. If a person was absent and we did not know why, we sent them an MIA letter. First-time guests were sent a letter, an email, and, later in the week, received a phone call. Those who returned a second or third time also received a letter. By the time a person or family had come a second or third time, I usually took them out for a meal after a Sunday service. During that visit, I acquired information about them, endeavoring to integrate them into a program at the church. I strongly believe that pastors are talent scouts, as they must constantly look for ways to help people in the church discover their spiritual gifts. This is especially true with people who are first joining the church.

Church Leadership

In September, I started a church leadership course, which met once a month following the morning worship service. We served pizza and provided childcare for each of the meetings. We invited anyone who had a job at the church along with anyone who might be interested in a job. I found an excellent book to use as a discussion guide: *Beyond the First Visit—The Complete Guide to Connecting Guests to Your Church* by Gary L. McIntosh. I ordered twenty copies and gave one to each family at the leadership meeting that first Sunday. Approximately twenty people attended these meetings. During the meeting, we discussed one chapter in the book. Many military personnel started attending the church services and these leadership meetings. There were two benefits of having the military in our congregation: (1) they are used to taking orders and are very respectful to leadership, and (2) I did not have to worry about security. At least twelve combat-trained military personnel attended our services! I was always amazed at the ideas that came from this group, especially regarding reaching people outside the church.

Guests are a Gift

Every Sunday, I emphasized the importance of treating first-time guests as very important people. I feel strongly that every first-time guest is actually a gift from God. We should treat them just as Jesus would treat them—greet them in the parking lot, greet them at the front door, give them a gift and a name tag, introduce them to several other people, tell them where everything is located, serve them a drink and a snack, and help them find a comfortable seat.

During friendship time, I encouraged each person to greet everyone else in the building. This meant that first-time guests might be greeted by twenty or more people. This would take a few minutes and was noisy, but very profitable. Following the service, we encouraged everyone to stay for snacks and drinks. Approximately 80 percent of first-time guests would join us. This was another great time to welcome our guests. We only have one time to make a good first impression, so we must take advantage of every opportunity.

One of our first breakthroughs had to do with a military family who visited the church. The three children were eight, ten, and twelve. The parents had decided to visit three churches in the area before making a decision regarding which church to attend. Ours was the first church. Parents and children measure the success of the children's church program in different ways. Parents want to see their children bring home some sort of project. Children measure success if they get a snack. As the family discussed their church experience, it led the parents to talk about the next two churches they would try next. However, the children said that their experience in the children's program was so good that they had found home...and that is how it turned out! The mother became one of our best greeters, and the family stayed in the church until they were transferred—two years after Joy and I left. They were the best; they brought excitement to each of our services. Two years after I left, I was invited back as a guest speaker. It was the last Sunday before this family moved to another location. In my prayer of blessing, I mentioned that there is a church out there that will be very fortunate when this family walks through their doors. Treat every first-time guest as a gift from God!

Celebrate Achieved Goals

It is also important to set goals. We set our first attendance goal at fifty for a regular service. We occasionally had more than fifty people—on Easter Sunday, a combined service with our Samoan fellowship, or on the Sunday we dedicated our remodeled buildings. Not only did we set the goal but agreed to have a steak BBQ with all the trimmings on the Sunday after reaching the goal. We achieved our goal on the third Sunday in September with fifty-six people in attendance. The following Sunday, we did have the BBQ, and the attendance was fifty-seven. Celebrate as often as you can. Make your goals realistic and get the whole group working together to reach that goal.

14. Another Fine Example

Most of us have been first-time guests at a church before. Joy and I had one of our best experiences ever while traveling by car from the Midwest to our home in California. Sunday morning, we were in my wife's birth town, Albuquerque, New Mexico. I wanted to see how this historic church was doing. We found its location and drove to their new facilities. As we approached the church, a greeter was holding a sign just as we entered the parking lot. The sign said, "First-time guests turn on your lights." Therefore, we did. The greeter introduced himself and asked for our names. He said they had a special parking spot for us and, on his mobile transmitter, called the greeter at the bottom of the parking lot saying, "This is Richard and Joy and they are our first-time guests." As we approached the second greeter, he led us to a special parking spot near the entrance to the church. He introduced himself and, after we parked the car, talked with us until we reached the outside of the auditorium. He then introduced us to the greeter at the door: "This is Richard and Joy and they are our first-time guests." The third greeter took us inside, explained the layout of the building, pointed out the coffee area and the location of the restrooms, and took us to the entrance of the auditorium. Once again, she introduced us to greeter number four. The fourth greeter escorted us in and helped us find a seat.

After the service was over, we walked to find our car. The second usher remembered our names. By now, they knew we were from California and would most likely not be returning. Nevertheless, it made no difference in how they treated us. As we were driving away, Joy said, "You know, if we were looking for a church home, our search would have just ended." It is no wonder this church holds two Sunday morning services, with an attendance of about one thousand in each service. We must remember that we only have one chance to make a good first impression.

Meeting Needs

It is important to look at your church and community and ask God to help you discern the needs in both areas. In our military town, it soon became obvious. Military spouses can oftentimes be very lonely. They are generally young, have moved from another area of the country, and their spouse is sometimes deployed or out in field training for long periods of time. Generally, the spouses are women, and some have small children who are not in school. Our first small group was a ladies Bible study and luncheon. Our first one was in August with an attendance of six. One of the purposes of the group was to provide fellowship. We hired a childcare worker so that ladies with children could relax with other ladies. The Bible study was a video series with nationally known speakers. It was really a simple program: start at 10:30 a.m., with lunch at noon, and then they could stay as long as they wished for fellowship. Many times, the ladies were still visiting at 1:30–2:00 p.m. It was an instant success. However, we did set an initial attendance goal of fifteen ladies.

The ladies' Bible study was important for another reason, which tied into our Sunday morning service. We could easily identify first-time guests on Sunday morning because of the nametags. Some of the ladies who regularly attended the ladies' Bible study on Tuesday took the opportunity to invite ladies who were first-time guests to the Bible study. Sometimes ladies needed more than one invitation. However, when a church lady sensed that a guest would most likely benefit from the Bible study, they extended the invitation again.

We reached our first goal of fifteen on my wife's birthday in November. Normally, we celebrated with a potluck, except that first-time guests were invited to be someone's guest. This Tuesday, I had lunch catered to celebrate my wife's birthday, and it became a second celebration since we had reached our attendance goal. Therefore, we set our next goal for twenty. Don't become discouraged if you do not reach your goals in a short period. For the next five months, we would sometimes break our record attendance of fifteen, but not reach our goal of twenty. Finally, in April, we reached our goal of twenty with twenty-three in attendance. The Bible instructs us not to become weary in doing well, but in the proper season, we will reach our goals *if* we do not give up.

Use the Ideas of Other People

Emma was just eighteen years old when she first came to church in September. She was engaged to Chaz, who was in the military. She asked me if I did premarital counseling, which I answered in the affirmative. I performed their marriage ceremony the next month. Emma was full of life and always had great ideas. She came from a great family and church. I had only known her about a month when she said, "Pastor, back home for Halloween, we used to have a Hallelujah Festival. Could we do that here?" Our Sunday attendance was in the fifties by then, and with just two weeks until Halloween, I thought we would not have enough time to prepare for the event. However, I could not say no to Emma. With fifty people in attendance on Sundays, I thought twenty people might show up—but I did not share those thoughts with Emma.

Emma went to work, and we had game booths, lots of food, including BBQ, and a hayride. About one hundred people showed up and I still do not know how they found out about it. I wondered if there would be any benefit the next Sunday. The previous weeks' attendance was forty-seven; the Sunday following the Hallelujah Festival, the attendance was sixty-three, with twenty-nine first-time guests! One family that was introduced to the church through the Hallelujah Festival has been in the church for three years now. The church gave Chaz and Emma a surprise wedding shower that day. It was a great Sunday. The pastor who followed me has continued the tradition, and last Halloween, one thousand people attended the Hallelujah Festival. And, yes, Chaz and Emma stayed in the church until they were transferred to Japan. One of our great American leaders said, "We have nothing to fear but fear itself." Celebrate often and have special events to reach the people of your community.

Preparing to Leave

Joy and I knew that our time at the church was limited because we had accepted a missions assignment to teach at a seminary in Baguio, Philippines. Knowing we had a limited timeframe, I began to set goals for the church to reach before we left. I wanted it to be averaging seventy-five people in Sunday morning attendance, with a weekly offering averaging $2,000. My membership goal was forty, and I wanted half of the church attendance to be coming from the military base.

First-Time Guest Assimilation

It is important not only to set goals but also to keep accurate records as you move toward those goals. Even though I was keeping track of many of our goals and numbers, I was not keeping track of our first-time guest assimilation rate. How many first-time guests became second-time attendees within the first month? Church leaders tell us that getting a first-time guest back the second time is 80 percent of the work of getting them to join the church. I was familiar with the statistics. A healthy church would have 5 percent of their attendance as first-time guests. In other words, if you had an attendance of one hundred, there should be five first-time guests. In addition, a healthy church should have a conversion rate of 15–20 percent of first-time guests to second-time attendees. The highest assimilation rate I have read about was a church that hit 74 percent, but it took a painful two- to three-year process.

The assimilation rate was 7 percent when I started measuring in November. In December, it went up to 21 percent. Then something miraculous happened. The assimilation rate for five months, from January through May, averaged 74 percent! The assimilation rate only included individuals who could potentially return. One might ask, "Did measuring the assimilation rate of first-time guests to second-time attendees make the church more successful in assimilating guests?" I am sure a number of contributing factors influenced the retention, so it is hard to determine if measuring actually increased effectiveness. However, less than 1 percent of churches measure that high of assimilation rate. Tracking the assimilation rate is hard work, but I believe it pays eternal dividends.

Continued Growth

We reached all our goals and had eighteen military families attending the church. The pastor who followed me is very gifted and continues these church growth principles. As the church continued to grow, they started a second morning worship service; within two years, they reached a high of 257 on Easter Sunday, with a yearly budget of $275,000. Remember from Scripture that one plants, one waters, and God gives the increase.

CHAPTER SIX

WHERE TO BEGIN

SOMETIMES STARTING SEEMS LIKE half the battle. This chapter will provide suggestions on how you can start laying out your church growth program. You can compare setting goals to doing what is necessary to reach those goals. For instance, if you decide you would like to net one person a week as your attendance goal, what steps do you need to implement to make it happen? If you net one person per week, at the end of the year, your church attendance will have increased by fifty. If you keep that up for ten years, your attendance would be at least five hundred people. Netting one person a week seems easy, but it can be hard work.

15. Physical Facility

Carl F. George believes that a major "step in implementing vision is to tackle the blockage problem." Church leadership should first analyze the current facility to identify things that could serve as a hindrance to growth. For instance, people often choose not to attend a church if they don't have adequate parking. George, in identifying this superficial, yet important, issue, believes that "your most crucial capacity determiner stems from your parking availability, not your seating capacity." The average car carries two people when it arrives at church. Therefore, if the church auditorium seats 120 people, the parking lot should accommodate sixty parking spaces. If the church plans for continued growth, it must maintain a ratio of one parking space for every 1.75 to 2 people in attendance. Parking plays a critical role in church attendance; no matter how many other things the church does correctly, it will never outgrow its parking capacity.

Another obstruction to church growth is the failure to have the buildings and restrooms handicapped accessible. According to the U.S. Census Bureau, 9 percent of the American public have difficulty walking or climbing stairs; or use a wheelchair, cane, crutches, or walker. This may be especially true when meeting in temporary facilities, which may not be built according to the Americans with Disabilities Act. Also, in older church buildings, the codes when they were built may not have required handicapped accessibility. If you fail to make your facilities handicapped accessible, you may exclude 9 percent of those who wish to attend your church.

A significant barrier to growth exists regarding the church's facilities. Many church consultants subscribe to the 80 percent capacity rule. Nelson Searcy, on the other hand, believes that people consider a church full when it is filled to 70 percent capacity. If an auditorium, on average, is filled to more than 70–80 percent of its capacity, Americans feel overcrowded. Church attendees may be willing to worship in very tight seating arrangements a few Sundays a year (Easter and Christmas); however, over a period of time, they may decide to go elsewhere. Searcy observes that, as church leaders, we love full rooms, so we say, 'Pack 'em in; there are still a few seats!' But the truth is that when a room reaches 70 percent of its seating capacity, it's full. Period. People stop inviting their friends because they perceive there is no more room. Some regular attendees stop coming because it's hard to find a seat.

Another facility concern centers on the size of the auditorium compared to the size of supporting rooms, especially for nursery and children's activities. An obstacle can arise when the auditorium seats two hundred people, but the nursery and other rooms for children only accommodate ten children. If a church desires to attract young families, it must provide ample room for nursery care and children's ministry.

A church must find creative ways of overcoming barriers pertaining to their facilities. For example, a church could add another service on Saturday or Sunday, neighboring businesses might allow people to park in their parking lot during service times, staff and some members could park farther away and be shuttled to the church. George suggests an innovative solution:

> If you are short on Sunday school space, install two Sunday school sessions, one before and one after the worship. If your auditorium is small, then offer two worship services with Sunday school in between. If you are tight all the way around, think about holding Sunday school and worship simultaneously. Send everybody from the first hour home and then repeat the process for the second hour. By creatively using your existing space without enlargement, you can increase your membership by 50 percent or better.

While issues pertaining to a church facility seem petty, the American culture demands quality facilities that will comfortably accommodate people so they don't feel overcrowded or inconvenienced. Therefore, the church cannot ignore the importance of providing an environment that extends a warm welcome to both guests and regular attendees.

16. Closing the Back Door

It is true that for any church to grow, it must convert first-time guests into second-time attendees. However, if every time someone joins the church a regular attendee leaves, there would never be an increase in attendance. In an average church, 6 percent of attendees leave each year. Your goal could be to cut that to 3 percent. The first thing to make that happen is to know who is attending the morning service. Keeping track of attendance is essential to closing the back door. Try to have a close enough relationship with regular attendees that they let someone in the leadership know if they are going to be absent. If a person is absent one week and you do not know why, send them an MIA letter. If they are absent a second week, contact them personally. Second, contact regular attendees at least every three months. Generally, I would contact regular attendees by phone and ask them if they had a particular need I could add to my prayer list. You could even pray with them over the phone. I would then place these requests in our church prayer request list. This process creates a conduit for regular attendees to have a conversation with the pastor. Third, call regular attendees on their birthdays and anniversaries. Fourth, be sure to contact them with flowers following a hospital stay or a loss in their family. Each week, meet with your leadership team and find out what is happening in the lives of those who regularly attend the church. Implementing these strategies will keep your back door closed.

17. Facilitating the Retention of First-Time Guests

Assimilation helps the church provide an easy but thoughtful process, whereby a first-time guest becomes a fully engaged and responsible member of the body of Christ. Assimilation of new members into the local church creates a sustainable growth pattern for the church as well as the individual. The implementation of assimilation strategies in the local church will result in healthy growth that comes by way of new converts rather than transfer growth.

Proverbs 18:24 declares, "A true friend sticks by you like family" (MSG). Generally speaking, first-time guests come to church seeking friends. Clarensau poses two thought-provoking questions: "What would happen if a church acted like Jesus? How would their experience of us change if they came in our doors and felt like we wanted them to be there?" People attend church because they long to make a connection with other people. This being the case, it begs the question: Why do people have such difficulty making connections when both the church and the individual generally want the same thing? Tim Dolan articulates the harsh reality:

> I have never come across a congregation that bills itself as the "unfriendly church." Every congregation likes to think of themselves as friendly and welcoming to visitors. And yet, from my own experience and from talking to others, I have found that churches are not always as welcoming to first-time visitors as they like to think they are.

Intentionality in Plan

Church leaders must create intentional avenues through which to welcome first-time guests. This intentional approach begins before the guest even arrives at the church. The church's website, for instance, should be geared for people who log onto the site for the first time by readily providing services times, directions to the church, and a means by which the person can contact the church via email and/or phone.

The intentionality of the church starts from the moment the first-time guest pulls into the parking lot and continues until he or she becomes a part of the body of Christ and joins the church as a member. The church should also provide signs so that as first-time guests approach the church property, they can easily locate the church entrance. Dolan created a friendly environment for first-time guests by dedicating three front row parking spaces for visitors. He believes this accomplishes two goals: "It made it easier for visitors to find a parking space in an otherwise full parking lot. Even more importantly, it communicated, in a very tangible way, that we expect visitors each Sunday. Visitors are important enough to us to have their own dedicated parking space."

First-time guests represent part of the treasury that God gives to a local church. Searcy says: "Did you have any first-time guests at your church last week? Those guests were God's gift to you. How did you receive them? Did you show the Giver your appreciation? Did you treat those gifts as they deserved to be treated by having a plan in place to integrate them into the life of your church?" Preparing for assimilation is the key to being successful in reaching the people God sends to your church. The Bible declares, "Well done, good and faithful servant! You have been faithful with a few things. I will put you in charge of many things" (Matt. 25:21). When the church prepares to welcome first-time guests, God will certainly send first-time guests to those services. Creating an assimilation plan requires study regarding effective processes, as well as trial and error, as one develops a plan for reaching the people God sends to the church. W. Edwards Deming states: "It is not enough to do your best; you must know what to do and then do your best." Part of any new program includes implementation as well as adjustments along the way to make the plan fit the unique needs of the church. Identifying effective assimilation programs based on successful models definitely makes sense.

Identify First-Time Guests

Searcy indicates that a healthy church should expect five guests for every one hundred regular attendees. A church should anticipate guests and focus on identifying each new person who attends the church. When a church has first-time guests but fails to create a plan for identifying the guests, it willfully allows a valuable person to quietly slip through the cracks without making a connection to the church.

The Communication Card

Research indicates that the use of a communication or connection type of card provides the most effective means for identifying first-time guests. At some point in the service, a church leader asks everyone to complete this card. Some churches insert the card into the weekly bulletin while other churches distribute the card during the service. Usually, first-time guests prefer not to be singled out from regular attendees; thus, everyone is encouraged to fill out the communication card. Rick Warren, based on his experience, learned that "when people feel self-conscious, they raise their emotional defenses. Since we want to communicate to the unchurched, our first task is to reduce their anxiety so that they drop their defenses."

When correctly implemented, churches find that approximately 80 percent of first-time guests will turn the card in at the appropriate time. Churches create many interesting ways to encourage people to fill out the communication card. Some churches make it a fun time during the service, while others offer a gift (like a Starbucks card) to the person whose communication card is drawn. Clarensau observes:

> The gift should be viewed as the first step toward an intentional relationship. By giving the church my contact information, I am yielding my anonymity and expressing my willingness for the connection to continue. Those who do so to receive a gift have demonstrated that any reluctance they feel about being known is smaller than their desire for the free gift.

Setting the technique aside, the goal is to collect as many communication cards as possible.

Dale Carnegie, in his classic work, *How to Win Friends and Influence People*, helps leaders identify means for influencing the behaviors and attitudes of other people. Therefore, leaders must attempt to put themselves in the place of a first-time guest and make them feel comfortable in this new environment. Carnegie suggests the following ideas: (1) be sincere—do not promise anything you cannot deliver; (2) know exactly what you want the other person to do—do not make them guess; (3) tell them what benefits they will receive when asking them to do something for you. Carnegie's principles readily apply to how churches treat first-time guests.

18. Who Are the First-time Guests, and What Are They Thinking?

Although it is always difficult to put yourself in someone else's place, one should make every attempt to do so. Roy Oswald made the following observation: "A crisis or transition usually propels an individual to go out and search for a church family. Fifty percent of those in our study had just geographically relocated and were looking for a suitable church in their new community." Based on that information, a church can construct a program that will make at least 50 percent of their first-time guests more comfortable. Often when people first relocate, they have not set up normal housekeeping activities. Dolan tells a very interesting story of how one couple used their gift of hospitality to welcome guests:

> One congregation I read about was able to identify two hundred people who joined that congregation primarily because one couple made it their ministry to invite visitors to brunch in their home. Here is the great thing about inviting people to brunch: it doesn't matter if they come or not. It is not actually eating the meal that makes the impression on visitors, but the fact that someone cared enough to invite them. Being invited to someone's home for a meal is the single best way I know to make a positive first impression.

That is important since a congregation only has one opportunity to make a first impression.

Since 50 percent of first-time guests have recently relocated, the church could prepare gifts that would help the first-time guests settle into their new community. For example, the church could provide "A Guide for New Residents." It could include referrals to professionals like doctors, dentists, lawyers, and accountants as well as local handymen, auto mechanics, or construction workers, and coupons to local businesses and restaurants. The guide should also include pertinent information about the ministries of the church.

When planning how to welcome first-time guests, make sure to include everyone in your congregation. In other words, create a team approach for this project. Laurie Beth Jones lists three things that a church needs to remember when endeavoring to get the whole church working together and behind important projects:

1. Keep things simple—reminding your team of the business they are really in.
2. Hold everyone responsible for customer satisfaction—making service the ultimate priority.
3. Release the genius of your team—freeing them to use their highest gifts.

Part of serving first-time guests well is making sure that everyone in the church understands that first-time guests are the key to continual and sustained growth in the church. Furthermore, Jones emphasizes the importance of turning work into a cause, as this helps people develop a passion for the task—even the task of welcoming first-time guests properly.

When first-time guests walk into the church, they can be some of the loneliest people on earth. Research conducted by George Gallup Jr. concludes that Americans are some of the loneliest people on the planet. How is that possible when three-fourths of Americans live in metropolitan areas and two-thirds of those Americans choose to live in the suburbs? American families and individuals participate in so many activities that the activities themselves keep people from forming the social contacts they really need. Consequently, the average family or single individual who has recently relocated felt somewhat lonely before he or she moved. Now, in the midst of a completely new environment, the loneliness seems exacerbated. The church can capitalize on meeting this lonely person's needs by helping the person feel wanted, loved, and respected. Randy Frazee, recognizing this need, encourages the church of the twenty-first century to "do more than add work to an already overbooked society; it must design new structures that help people simplify their lives and develop more meaning, depth, purpose, and community." The church must not smother or ignore their first-time guests but rather welcome them as if they were a guest in one's own home. Introduce the guests to other people with the thought of connecting the person to other individuals who may have a common interest. Offer guests refreshments, hand them a bulletin, and escort them to a seat. After the service, greet the guest by name, wish him or her a good day, and invite the person to come back next Sunday or to enjoy other ministries of the church.

The fragility of first-time guests cannot be overstated. Jonathan Gainsbrugh comments: "Ethology is the study of the repetitive, territorial, and habit-forming characteristics of people. Ethologically, the most fragile of all church-folk is the first-time guest." Gainsbrugh lists several ideas to help the first-time guest enjoy a stress-free encounter with the church: (1) establish first-time guest parking, (2) provide a hospitality and information booth by the main entrance, (3) place greeters at the doors to personally welcome first-time guests and help them know where to go, (4) greet guests after the service by hosting a visitor's reception where each guest receives a small gift, or where the guests have their photo taken, or a hospitality team hosts the first-time guest for lunch.

First-time guests are God's gift to the local church; therefore, the church should be ever mindful of treating a first-time guest as if Christ himself had entered the church. Elmer Towns, Ed Stetzer, and Warren Bird comment: "People bring their friends when they are excited about the church—they find it attractive and are convinced that others will as well." Matthew 25:40 declares, "Whatever you did for one of the least of these brothers of mine, you did for me." When an individual or church feeds the hungry, gives a drink to the thirsty, treats a stranger with kindness, gives a needy person clothing, or visits the sick or imprisoned, it is as if it was done unto Jesus himself. Christ promises to build his church, and when the church family welcomes first-time guests well, Christ nods with approval.

Develop a Plan for Ministering to First-Time Guests

An old adage declares, "If we fail to plan, we plan to fail." Bill Hybels recognizes the importance of creating a plan: "At a certain point, people need more than vision. They need a plan, a step-by-step explanation of how to move from vision to reality." Because first-time guests are so critical to the church's growth, one cannot leave this area of ministry to chance. Ed Stetzer emphasizes that each church should have a Welcome Coordinator who "organizes greeters, ushers, and other volunteers who make gathering with the church a warm and friendly experience for guests. Greeters help attendees feel welcomed and wanted. Volunteers must be able to tell arriving guests where to go and what to do." He highlights the importance of having friendly and knowledgeable volunteers who can meet every conceivable need—from the location of the restrooms and first-aid kit to the location of all the ministries of the church. Stetzer lists the tasks for greeters to consider:

1.   Greet first-time guests in the parking lot.
2.   Clearly mark all entrances.
3.   Provide name tags for all attendees.
4.   Assign "seat shepherds" who sit in a specific area each week to connect guests with nearby members to make them feel welcome.

A church must intentionally develop its greeters and ushers so this vital component of retention can help first-time guests feel a warm welcome when they attend the church. Gary McIntosh comments: "Find the people who are positive thinkers and give them opportunities to be cheerleaders."

The Role of First Impressions

Turning first-time guests into second-time attendees should be the goal of every church. Shweta L. Khare, from Career Brights, states: "'The first impression is the last impression,' may or may not be true, but first impressions last.... Within the first three seconds of a new encounter, you are evaluated ... even if it is just a glance." In coaching executives, Jill Bremer also emphasizes the importance of first impressions:

> Impressions are based upon instinct and emotion, not on rational thought or in-depth investigation. When you step into a room, people make subconscious decisions about you. Within about thirty seconds, they've judged your economic and educational levels, your social position, and your levels of sophistication and success. After about four minutes, they've also made decisions about your trustworthiness, compassion, reliability, intelligence, capability, humility, friendliness, and confidence.

The power of a first impression can never be overstated. Searcy presents a sobering thought: "Seven minutes is all you get to make a positive first impression. In the first seven minutes of contact with your church, your first-time guests will know whether they are coming back." Before the first-time guest participates in worship or listens to the sermon, the guest has decided whether he or she will come again. The worship and the sermon may validate their decision, but worship and the sermon alone will not be the determining factor on whether they return the following week.

The person subconsciously sizes up a multitude of issues as he or she makes a decision. Bremer, noting the complexity and power of the human subconscious, declares: "Most of us float through life unaware of its influence; our subconscious is constantly shaping our thoughts, experiences, reactions and opinions." In *Strangers to Ourselves: Discovering the Adaptive Unconscious*, Timothy D. Wilson makes the following observation:

> The mind operates most efficiently by relegating a good deal of high-level, sophisticated thinking to the unconscious, just as a modern jetliner is able to fly on automatic pilot with little or no input from the human, "conscious" pilot. The adaptive unconscious does an excellent job of sizing up the world in a sophisticated and efficient manner.

Since individuals quickly make evaluations, church people must prepare for encounters with first-time guests. The procedures for welcoming first-time guests in a way that will encourage them to become second-time attendees should be written out, well-planned, and flawlessly executed. Mark L. Waltz observes: "Before our guests arrive, we need to envision the experience we desire for them. If we can see that experience clearly, we can create a road map to lead them there." Since one cannot keep first-time guests from making quick decisions about the church, it behooves the church to capitalize on its understanding of first impressions and the role of the subconscious to create an effective means of welcoming first-time guests. The goal is to increase the retention rate of first-time guests with the ultimate goal of moving them to become both followers of Christ and members of the church.

Statistically speaking, eight out of ten churches score poorly when it comes to their treatment of first-time guests. First impressions are so critical that the church must get it right the first time. When churches understand the intrinsic value of first impressions, first-time guests will be more inclined to attend a second time. Therefore, the church must purposely choose to make first-time guests a high priority to experience greater first-time guest retention.

First-time guests do not focus on making logical decisions based on the sermon's theological correctness or the type of worship. The first-time guest subconsciously measures the church's mood and the friendliness of the people they have encountered. In light of this information, Searcy summarizes four components of the pre-service: (1) Greeted—welcome guests with a smile; (2) Directed—simply and politely show the guests where they should go; (3) Treated—show the guest respect, and surprise them with comfort food or drink; (4) Seated—lead the guest to comfortable and appropriate seating.

At a rudimentary level, first-time guests assess the grass, the parking lot, the signs, and the overall appeal of the building. Knowing the importance of appearances, church leaders should strive to make their facilities look as good as possible. It is the first opportunity for the church to do more than what the first-time guest expects by investing 100 percent effort into this task. Waltz comments: "To be a 'Wow!' an experience must be unexpected." Simple touches, such as providing directional arrows, a flower garden or a water fountain, can create a "wow" factor that captures the persons' attention. Highlighting one area can illustrate how much the church cares about the first-time guests' perspective of the church. One county required a new church to include extensive landscaping. Initially, the church chaffed at the extra expense; however, the church received the "Desert Beautiful Award" for three years due to its striking beauty.

Once the first-time guests have entered the church building, the greeter will make the most important impression on the first-time guest. McIntosh comments, "Initial contacts with people play a major role in guests' thoughts about a church. Are church members outgoing and approachable?" The greeter should know how to smile, as nothing can replace an infectious smile. Smiling can actually be taught, and some churches even have smile warm-ups before the church service begins. Paul Ekman, Professor Emeritus of the Department of Psychiatry at the University of California Medical School in San Francisco, declares: "We can pick up a smile from thirty meters away. A smile lets us know that we are going to get a positive reception and it's hard not to reciprocate." While smiling plays an important role, greeters must be genuinely friendly people, so select people who already demonstrate that attribute.

Giving first-time guests more than what they expected is the key to encouraging them to be second-time attendees. Rainer talks about interviewing a couple at one of his study churches in Florida. Their expectations had been far exceeded. Rainer records their conversation as follows:

> When we arrived at the Sunday school class, a couple met us at the door. They talked with us and introduced us to others. Then they sat with us during the Sunday school. After Sunday school, they asked if they could sit with us during the worship service. We just left them a few minutes ago and they've invited us to lunch next Sunday.

Rainer goes on to comment about the effectiveness of the well-organized greeter ministry of the Florida church: "Even the greeters in the Sunday school class are trained to sit with visitors and to ask to sit with them in worship services. And the church offers to reimburse any member who takes a first-time guest to lunch."

Many first-time guests hold prejudices or preconceived notions regarding the church. Oftentimes, first-time guests have visited several other churches. Searcy identifies the challenges of meeting the needs of first-time guests: "Most of the people who walk through your door have been burned by the church, by negative press about the church, or by a friend or family member in the name of religion." Therefore, church leaders must find ways to overcome possible prejudices of first-time attendees. Potentially, the first-time guest did not receive a warm welcome at another church. Although not a business seeking to make a profit, the church can encourage repeat business by learning from successful business principles. Ken Blanchard, in *Raving Fans: A Revolutionary Approach to Customer Service*, shares three secrets for planning for repeat customers. One of the secrets that can significantly help church leaders is to "deliver your vision plus 1 percent."

The church can help break down prejudices and preconceived notions by providing a guest reception where the guests can partake of simple foods, such as coffee, milk, and a light snack. Amazingly, food has the ability to make a first-time guest feel comfortable and at home. Simply holding a cup of coffee or a cup of water in one's hand while with a crowd of unknown people can make a person feel at ease. Food is one thing that all people have in common; therefore, it can break down barriers and make a person feel more relaxed.

When serving food, always plan generously. Do not limit the food to first-time guests but make it available to everyone who comes to the guest reception, as this encourages the first-time guest to join the group by enjoying the food. McIntosh observes: "A staff reception for new guests helps people gain some basic knowledge of the church and staff." This is the church's opportunity to welcome its guests, so never charge a fee or provide a receptacle for donations. Utilizing the first seven minutes effectively can dramatically increase visitor retention.

Creative Ways of Providing Food, Coffee, and Snacks

Jesus understood the importance of fellowship and food. His first miracle was at a wedding where he turned the water into wine. The Scripture tells us the importance of taking care of our own families, along with others like orphans and widows who may be less fortunate than ourselves. We are also told that sometimes we might be entertaining angels and not even be aware of it. The Bible often mentions food and, of course, all of us must eat. Remember how Jesus took care of large groups of people because he saw their need to be fed? At different times in the Bible, God miraculously provided food.

One way of providing food for first-time guests and other meal functions at church is to include it in the church budget. If you are trying to provide coffee and donut holes for fifty people each week, you should be able to do it for fifty cents per person. If you get creative, you may be able to provide a meal for your leadership meeting for a dollar per person. One way to reduce the cost is to serve pizza from Costco, Sam's, or a discount store. My daughter is in charge of providing lunch for 250 teenagers at the Fellowship of Christian Athletics each week at her daughter's high school. A local fast-food restaurant gives a 50 percent discount, and the bill is usually less than $150. Volunteers sometimes provide fried chicken from a supermarket and, occasionally, a nearby restaurant provides an entire meal at no charge.

At one church, we asked volunteers to sign up to provide snacks one Sunday a month for three months. This had two benefits: (1) more people from the church began participating, and some individuals really enjoyed the opportunity to provide the snacks, and (2) it kept the general fund from having to pay the bill. One couple enjoyed it so much that they would back their SUV up to the church just to unload all they brought. They probably brought enough food for at least a couple of weeks. Volunteers only signed up for three months at a time to keep them from feeling overwhelmed. They were not required to make a lifelong commitment; they simply committed themselves to three times in the next three months. Then we would start all over, which gave other people an opportunity to participate. When your goal is to involve 60 percent of the people attending the church, it makes it possible for more people to participate. Many ministries are available, especially for those who may not enjoy being up front or in a public ministry.

I suppose that since the very beginning, the church has implemented the pot-luck concept! Each person or family is asked to participate by bringing a certain food dish. Churches creatively find ways of suggesting who brings what type of food to ensure variety at the meal. Most growing churches have food as part of their culture—a Bible pattern!

Planning for the Return of First-Time Guests

Turning first-time guests into second-time attendees should be the goal of every church. The follow-up for first-time guests should begin soon after the guests leave the Sunday morning service, but no later than Monday. Although assimilation rates vary from church to church, Rainer conducted a study of 287 churches to identify visitor retention rates. His study focused on identifying the percentage of first-time guests who returned for a second visit. His results indicate the following:

Lower-assimilation churches in the study	50.8%
Higher-assimilation churches in the study	74.4%
All churches in the study	62.6%

All churches aspire to be high-assimilation churches, but Rainer summarizes, in one word, how a church can become a high-assimilation church: expectations. Rainer lists three comments by visitors regarding high-assimilation churches:

1. "Unlike some other churches we visited, this church seemed to act like the Christian faith really mattered."
2. "We were met by greeters everywhere we turned. We never lost our way. It is easy to see that this church expects a lot of it members."
3. "Everything about the church told me that the people cared, that they took their faith seriously."

The high-assimilation churches were the high-expectation churches. First-time guests understood that God truly meant something to the attendees, and members took their jobs very seriously. Furthermore, the first-time guests understood that membership in that church meant something. If they were to become members, they would also be assigned something to do at the church.

Not all first-time guests are likely to be second-time attendees in the near future. However, all first-time guests should be treated well.

The church should categorize first-time guests based on their location to the church. All churches have first-time guests who may be out-of-town guests of members or were passing through and dropped in to attend a service. The church should send out-of-town guests a letter, email, or another form of communication thanking them for their attendance, and, if they gave a gift, acknowledging their gift. The letter should also invite the guest to return to the church the next time they are in the area. Often first-time guests will return to an out-of-town church for another visit if they were treated well. One never knows if the guest plans to relocate to the area in the near future.

The church should create a well-thought out plan for contacting first-time guests who could potentially return for a second visit. Searcy lists three things to consider when constructing a follow-up plan for first-time guests: (1) fast, (2) friendly, and (3) functional. The current generation expects fast service; therefore, while still fresh in their minds, the visitors should receive multiple contacts from the church starting on the Monday following their Sunday visit. The communication with the first-time guest should be friendly, personal, and warm, yet functional. The visitor packet provided should provide simple, straightforward, and useful information, including a genuine invitation to return to the next service. Including a small surprise would exceed the guests' expectations.

Churches use a variety of ways for following up with their first-time guests. Rainer indicates that "99.1 percent of the high-assimilation churches had a systematic plan for visitor follow-up." Some churches begin the follow-up by inviting their first-time guests to a meal following the morning service. Other churches suggest that people visit the guest at their home on Sunday afternoon. Despite the variety of plans, almost all churches plan to begin with a contact on

Monday. Churches that are most effective in follow-up to first-time guests make four contacts the first week. The contact information can be gathered from the following sources: (1) communication card, (2) children's check-in information, or (3) offering records—if the guest gave by check, generally the check will include their name and address, or if they used the offering envelope, it might include their contact information.

The first contact should be made by email or a text message if an email address or phone number is available. Searcy's research indicates that the best time for the email to arrive is between 2 and 3 p.m. on Monday as, by that time, the person will have read their other weekend email and might be getting a little bored by that time of the day. The email should be friendly, informing the first-time guest about an upcoming church event along with an invitation to attend the church in the near future. Searcy also uses a first-time guest online survey with four questions: (1) What did you notice first? (2) What did you like best? (3) What was your overall impression? (4) How can we pray for you?

The next contact should be a personal phone call. Keep this call simple; this is not the time to gather a complete history of the family. The third contact should be a handwritten note to the first-time guest simply thanking them for their attendance, offering to help in any way, and inviting them to attend church the next Sunday. The fourth contact should be a personal visit to the home with a small gift, such as homemade cookies. This visit should only last about thirty seconds at the door. If no one is home, leave a personal note along with the gift. Rainer observes: "Almost every church in my study insisted on a personal follow-up visit by the pastor, other staff, or a layperson. A visit from a layperson was deemed most effective by the visitors we interviewed; however, a pastor was involved in personal visits 67.6 percent of the time." Using the four contact methods described above should result in 74 percent of first-time guests becoming second-time attendees.

One can send a one-month follow-up letter to individuals who did not return after their first visit. The unchurched are not used to going to church on Sunday. They may have been perfectly happy with the service and the treatment they received. However, their Sundays already have a full schedule of events and, for them, attending once a month may seem normal. Clarensau says: "Contacts should be ongoing. The church should not assume that a guest who plans to return will always do so the following week." A one-month follow-up letter shows that the church really does care about them. Include a gift like a CD or a small gift card. Searcy comments: "When you make the effort to contact them a month later, not only do you remind them of their initial experience, but you also show them that they matter to you. It is a level of connection they are not expecting but will be glad to receive."

Persistence is important in bringing people to faith. The business world understands how important it is to be persistent in winning new business. Thomas S. Argyle, vice-president of sales for Union Oil, held the responsibility of winning major accounts for his company. When he went after a major account, he kept going back until he obtained the account. He was asked, "What happens if you keep going back and they never sign up?" He thought for a moment and said, "That never happened." Jesus taught about the importance of importunity when he encouraged his followers to be persistent when asking for something with a good and noble goal (Luke 11:8). Quite honestly, a church rarely makes too many contacts.

19. Effective Assimilation of First-Time Guests into the Local Church

Once the first-time guest becomes a second-time attendee, the church leader must focus on the process of bringing that person to the saving knowledge of Jesus, if that commitment has not already been made, and introducing the individual to members of the local church. Searcy observes: "When your guests return for a second look, you've won 80 percent of the battle of gaining new regular attendees and have drastically increased the chances that they will begin a journey with Christ." Sometimes friends pressure a first-time guest to come to church, but when the first-time guest comes the second time, it is based on a personal choice. Church leaders should be grateful to God when a person comes back a second time, as it indicates God's reward for diligent retention efforts. When church leaders partner with God to reach the unchurched, they can expect a significant harvest.

When a person comes back a second time, it indicates that the assimilation plan works. People come to church for the first time for many reasons; when they come back a second time, they are looking for relationships with other people. They enter the church the second time hoping that someone will remember them as a person and maybe even remember their name. Gainsbrugh says: "If a visitor is remembered the following week when he returns as a second-time guest, he or she may give you 'ten points.' However, if a greeter somehow remembers their name and face, it gets the 'gold ring' or twenty-five points of 'bonding glue.'" The best way to help the greeter remember a person's name is to have multiple contacts with that person. When a church is staffed with the correct number of greeters, each greeter has more time to take a personal interest in the first-time guest. Remembering someone is a key point to helping the second-time attendee know that building a relationship at this "new church" is a possibility. Rainer theorizes, "When assimilation takes place in a church, the pastor, staff, and other leaders are working fervently. Effective assimilation requires hard work. And the leaders must be visibly at the forefront of the efforts."

Effective assimilation requires knowing who attended the morning worship service and having a well-thought-out program to reach each person who came as both a first- and second-time guest. Gary McIntosh and Glen Martin, in their book, *Finding Them, Keeping Them: Effective Strategies for Evangelism and Assimilation in the Local Church*, list four ways to effectively assimilate new attendees into the local church: (1) assimilation through friendship, (2) assimilation through tasks/roles, (3) assimilation through small groups, (4) assimilation through spiritual growth.

Assimilation through Friendship

While one cannot have too many friends, if a person has one true friend in life, he or she is fortunate indeed. Most people long for a true friend. Therefore, one of the most important things a church can offer people seeking a new place of worship is friendship. Ralph Waldo Emerson said: "A friend is a person with whom I may be sincere. Before him I may think aloud. A friend may well be reckoned the masterpiece of nature." McIntosh and Martin state: "Assimilation begins right at the heart of our need for relationship." Church leaders must help new people in the church move from casual friendships to relational friendships where they experience a sense of belonging and accountability. When the local church does not help new attendees transition into meaningful friendships, people live with an unmet need. Alan Loy McGinnis makes a sobering observation:

People with no friends usually have a diminished capacity for sustaining any kind of love. They tend to go through a succession of marriages, be estranged from various family members, and have trouble getting along at work. On the other hand, those who learn how to love their friends tend to make long and fulfilling marriages, get along well with the people at work, and enjoy their children.

Church leaders must understand the importance of creating an environment in which new attendees can easily make new friends in the congregation. Win Arn and Charles Arn indicate that each person needs at least seven friends in order to stay in a church. When people find a true friend at church, they willingly sacrifice for one another while also enjoying the mutual benefits of nurturing one another spiritually.

Assimilation through Tasks/Roles

In a perfect church, each member would have a specific task to accomplish. A task includes any job with kingdom purpose inside the church. Each member should only do one job; otherwise, fewer members will have the opportunity to participate in the ministries of the church. Carl S. Dudley believes that boredom serves as the primary reason for why people leave the church. Barna further emphasizes the importance of involvement when he poignantly states: "Unless you become involved in the activities of your church, you will never truly feel satisfied with that church." Win Arn, a church growth expert, provides a means by which to measure the importance of each person's involvement in the church. Performing tasks not only ensures the accomplishment of kingdom work but also ties individuals doing the tasks to one another. Arn's research indicates that a declining church has twenty-seven tasks per one hundred people and that each individual usually performs more than one task. This, in essence, limits the total number of participants. A plateaued church reflects a ratio of forty-three tasks to one hundred people in attendance. However, growing and healthy churches demonstrate a ratio of sixty tasks for every one hundred people in attendance, with almost no one doing more than one task.

People should not be assigned tasks just for the sake of keeping them busy. Frank Tillapaugh, pastor of Bear Valley Baptist Church, observes that a healthy church creates jobs by looking for new opportunities for effective ministry. When the church serves as Jesus did, it reflects God's heart, for the "Son of Man did not come to be served, but to serve, and to give his life as a ransom for many" (Matt. 20:28). The apostle Paul also teaches about the importance of spiritual gifts and how everyone should participate in the ministry through the body of Christ: "Now to each one the manifestation of the Spirit is given for the common good. Just as a body, though one, has many parts, but all its many parts form one body, so it is with Christ. Now you are the body of Christ, and each one of you is a part of it" (1 Cor. 12:7, 12, 27). The old adage, "Many hands make light work," clearly applies in the context of the ministries of the church. Leaders must help congregants work together in the kingdom of Christ. A children's song summarizes this concept very well: "When we all pull together, together, together. When we all pull together, how happy we'll be. For your work is my work and our work is God's work; when we all pull together, how happy we'll be."

Assimilation through Small Groups

Groups of twelve to fifteen people provide the type of fellowship intrinsically needed for quenching the human need for community. The early church met regularly in homes for several centuries. Although the church cannot return to the era of the early church, their approach illustrates the importance of carving out time and creating opportunities for people to meet in small groups. McIntosh and Martin indicate that "church growth studies have found that for a church to assimilate new people effectively it must have an average of seven small groups for every one hundred adult members." Furthermore, they identify four essential ingredients that add to the assimilation mix: (1) sharing, (2) study, (3) support, and (4) service.

Sharing

Charles H. Spurgeon observed: "A good character is the best tombstone. Those who loved you, and were helped by you, will remember you when forget-me-nots are withered. Carve your name on hearts, and not on marble." A small group must create an environment where people can share on an intimate level. Whether an individual is facing difficult life circumstances or celebrating life's victories, a small group offers the community in which to express these situations. McIntosh and Martin comment: "We were created in God's image with a yearning to commune with God, and with other relational beings. We long to know and to be known on levels transcending the superficial plane." When we communicate on an intimate level, it enables believers to more easily fulfill the Scriptures' admonition to carry one another's burdens and, in this way, fulfill the law of Christ (Gal. 6:2). When a person shares the details of his or her life with a Christian friend, it not only serves as a catharsis for the person sharing but also encourages the listener to intercede for the friend's needs.

Study

As people study the Bible together, they become better followers of Christ. Dwight D. Eisenhower observed: "To read the Bible is to take a trip to a fair land where the spirit is strengthened and faith renewed." Towns, Stetzer, and Bird believe "discipleship best happens in community." When believers study God's Word together, they not only renew their minds but also permit the Spirit to challenge them for duties of service. Because of Bible study, people experience changes in every area of their lives. Their work ethic improves, and their minds are transformed. Consequently, the Spirit of God directs every part of their day. The daily renewal through the Word of God creates excitement, and individuals in the group are encouraged to a life of excellence through their corporate efforts.

Support

Providing support for a friend in need could require sacrificial giving. On other occasions, sharing valuable life experiences can help a friend realize he or she is not alone in life. William Feather comments: "Nothing happens to you that hasn't happened to someone else." As people become better acquainted, they more readily share experiences that help create a new filter for life. People long for genuine and loyal friends who will readily help during the difficult times of life. Christians, above all, should make sure their actions match their words, as that will lead to an abundance of friends.

Service

Genuine believers should exemplify the quality of service by meeting the needs of other people. As a small group, believers can accomplish extraordinary things for God. God himself makes an incredible promise to people who care for the less fortunate: "Mercy to the needy is a loan to God, and God pays back those loans in full" (Prov. 19:17 MSG). John Wesley said: "Do all the good you can, by all the means you can, in all the ways you can, in all the places you can, at all the times you can, to all the people you can, and as long as you can." New opportunities will present themselves as small group participants seek God's direction regarding service to people in need.

Assimilation through Spiritual Growth

Spiritual growth, like all growth, generally comes gradually over time. Individuals can encourage spiritual growth by purposely developing a Bible reading plan, participating in regular Bible study, and being in close association with people in a small group who also desire to grow spiritually. At the age of seventy-five, someone asked Henry Wadsworth Longfellow how he continued to write so well. He pointed to an apple tree full of blooms and said, "That is a very old apple tree, but the blossoms this year seem more beautiful than ever before. That old tree grows a little new wood each year, and I suppose it is out of the new wood that these blossoms come. Like the apple tree, I try to grow a little new wood each year."

God desires that every believer reach full maturity in Christ. If a believer stops growing spiritually, it indicates a separation from the source of life. Jesus expresses this relationship: "Live in me. Make your home in me just as I do in you. In the same way that a branch can't bear grapes by itself but only by being joined to the vine, you can't bear fruit unless you are joined with me" (John 15:4 MSG). Therefore, full maturity occurs as both the church and its individual members live in close connection to the Lord. Jesus' goal is to assimilate new members into the body of Christ and into the fellowship of a local church. Inside this protective setting, God's people receive encouragement, nourishment, and blessing.

CHAPTER SEVEN

GETTING READY FOR COMPANY
Should You Do This by Yourself?

REMEMBER THE OLD ADAGE, "Many hands make light work." It is a biblical concept for pastors to train upcoming leaders. Jesus spent most of his public ministry training his disciples for current and future ministries. Jesus instructs us to make disciples. Doing ministry alone is not fun, and it keeps leaders exhausted and church members frustrated. Most people who regularly attend church want to be involved in some type of ministry. The pastor must make sure they are both challenged and properly trained. Training cannot be a one-time event; it must be ongoing. I enjoyed having a leadership training session each month. Usually, we held this meeting after the Sunday morning worship service and involved a light lunch, like pizza, and included childcare.

Basically, by providing leadership training, the pastor is establishing a comprehensive guest retention program. For some churches, this will involve a cultural change, up to and including, a new paradigm. Almost all groups develop a unique culture. The group could be as large as a country or as small as a fellowship group.

The longer a group has been in existence, the more embedded the culture, and possibly the more difficult to change. When setting up a new program, it is important to understand at least two things. First, while one segment of a group may eagerly follow your leadership, a smaller portion of the group may require more attention to adapt to the change. I call this necessary step "education with purpose." For instance, when asking everyone to wear name tags every Sunday, inform them of the reason for this action. We basically tell them that if all of us do this, more people will be able to find Christ as their personal savior. We are demonstrating to the world that we care and love each other. Wearing name tags helps us call one another by name and is very important to accomplishing that goal. It will help us more easily identify our first-time guests and help us remember their names when they come back the next week.

Second, when you have good, noble, and godly goals that are clearly articulated, it is much easier for the group to begin to make the necessary changes in behavior. To accomplish our goals, we need to train more people to help with our guest retention program. We will need a director, someone able to train more ushers and greeters, someone in charge of the food ministry, and people who will be involved in contacting first-time guests after their visit. As you make the initial presentation, it would be a good time to let people sign up for these assignments.

How do you eat an elephant? One bite at a time. Start by getting a few leaders together and having them help make an outline of each job that needs to be done. Then, give a scriptural devotion and have a time of prayer to help inspire your leadership team for the tasks ahead. Once they see your passion and desire to have more people assimilated into God's kingdom, you are well on your way to success.

When a person is getting ready for company, it can take anywhere from an hour to several days. Launching a successful church growth program will usually take at least thirty days. Once you have determined that your facilities are the correct size for your attendance goals, the next thing is what I call the "WOW factor." When a person drives up to your facilities, is there something so nice that it is more than what they expected? On the outside, it might be a very attractive sign, a beautiful rose garden or great landscaping, an up-to-date play area for children, or some other eye-catching physical item. There might be an outside café or a group of friendly greeters. On the inside, it may be a lovely painting or an indoor fountain. Try to have at least one thing that would impress your first-time guests, showing that this church cares about its buildings, both inside and outside.

It is also very important that the outside be tidy and the inside be very clean. Restrooms should be up-to-date and handicapped accessible. If you are having two Sunday morning services, someone should have the responsibility of tidying up the restrooms and sanctuary between services. Since people do not arrive at your building at a predicable rate, always provide more than enough ushers and greeters. For instance, a family may arrive with children of different ages. It may take a greeter five minutes or more to take the family to the nursery, introduce them to the attendant, and get them signed in. Then they would need to take another child to the children's program and get them registered. In this case, more is better.

During the thirty-day period of preparing for guests, church leaders should recruit and train ushers and greeters. After proper instruction on how to greet and direct the first-time guests, I like to do role-playing. Have a couple of people play the role of being first-time guests. Then have the ushers and greeters-in-training help them while the rest of the people watch. Often, this is quite humorous, but it gets the message across. Then reverse the roles until everyone has had a chance to be greeters and ushers-in-training.

Another essential part of this program is having drinks and snacks available to everyone. Whenever weather permits, I like having the refreshments outside for a couple of reasons. It is very easy for the first-time guests to participate without going to another location. Second, as people drive up, they see a group of people just hanging out and having fellowship, which is very inviting. Let me mention that this is not the time to receive an offering. Do not have a place for people to "pay" for the refreshments. Any sign should say, "Complimentary Snacks."

Let me tell you about some things I tried that worked well. In addition to the snacks before, and possibly after, the service, have a snack time during the service. I have seen this done with churches of 50 to 2,500. Many churches have a time for people to greet one another. However, this is a more organized event that, generally speaking, should be done in seven minutes. The pastor announces it is time for fellowship and a snack break. Refreshments are located either at the back of the building or, with larger groups, around the inside perimeter of the sanctuary. We usually serve donut holes or bagels with coffee for the adults and possibly milk if the children are present. In smaller groups, this gives the lead pastor time to greet first-time guests. After about six minutes, music begins to play and the group is called back to order.

This is an aggressive approach but highlights the importance of greeting first-time guests and each another. If one implements this idea with an established group, one can expect to get a couple of complaints. Some individuals suggest that a break will interrupt the spiritual aspects of the service. In that case, I usually share a couple of poignant stories to quell the person's fears. This approach is not suitable for every church situation, but I have seen it work effectively over long periods of time.

Depending on the size of your property, station greeters at several locations. I like to have two greeters at each of the entrances to the parking lots. This is a great way to use your teenagers before the service begins. Provide each parking lot greeter an orange vest to wear along with some colorful gloves. Train the young people to smile and wave as cars begin to enter the parking lot. This should begin about fifteen minutes before service time and remain in place until fifteen minutes past starting time. If possible, use a sign that says: "Turn on flashers if you are a first-time guest." This will help your greeters identify first-time guests and direct them to the spaces near the front of the building marked "Guest Parking." If signs are not available, train greeters to "look" for first-time guests by noticing those who are unsure of where they should go and may be driving slowly. At one church, the teenage greeter was not directing the guests to the designated parking spaces. So I told him I would give him $5 for every guest he parked in the guest parking area. It worked!

At one church, there was quite a distance from the parking lot to the sanctuary. Therefore, I placed a greeter near the end of the parking area and the walkway that went up to the church. The greeter would greet each person and direct them toward the sanctuary. Whether using greeters or signs, the goal is to make it easy for first-time guests to find the entrance to your buildings.

In churches with less than one hundred people in attendance, it is fairly easy to identify first-time guests. Regardless of the number of weekly guests, I encourage churches to have a greeting table for first-time guests. I drape a table with a large tablecloth that displays the word "Guests" in very large letters. Place registration cards, pens, and a gift on the table. Do not wait until after the service to give gifts *if* they turn in a welcome card (see Appendix E). Many people will fill out the registration card there, receive a nametag, be introduced to three or four other people, and enjoy a light snack. If there is enough time, a greeter can give them a brief tour, help them find the children's area, if necessary, and then escort them into the auditorium. After the service is finished, it is important to invite first-time guests to a time of fellowship and refreshments. Second, take advantage of their desire to connect with people by providing small groups and Bible study options they can attend. For example, one could say: "We are having a Bible study this week on Tuesday at 6:30 p.m. We will be meeting in the fellowship hall and I would like you to be my guest. If you are not able to make that, it would be our pleasure to have you back next Sunday." If a lady is present, she should receive an invitation to the weekly ladies' Bible study, or a young person could be invited to the mid-week youth service, and so on. Third, have information readily available for the current Bible teaching events and invite the guest to attend. First-time guests come in a variety of spiritual maturities. Some individuals may come with significant church background while others may be seeking knowledge about God for the first time. Regardless of spiritual state, each person is created in the image of God and is seeking to be in community with a group.

As the church prepares for welcoming guests, they can begin using the registration cards four weeks prior to Launch Sunday. Each week, the office staff will enter the information into an electronic spreadsheet. The week before Launch Sunday, they will print nametags for all regular attendees. I recommend printing the first name as large as possible and the last name smaller but readable. Arrange the nametags on a table in alphabetical order. Greeters should arrive at least thirty minutes prior to the service time. Announce to regular attendees that fellowship and snacks will be available at 10 a.m. and the service will begin at 10:30 a.m. For the first service, plan to have extra greeters on duty because some names may be spelled incorrectly, and some individuals will need help with this new process. Hand write new nametags for any incorrect names and make the correction on the master name list. When making a nametag for a first-time guest, simply use the person's first name. Please be ready for a little confusion the first Sunday. A couple of people might resist the idea of wearing a nametag. If so, do not insist on them wearing one. You will find that by the second or third Sunday, almost everyone attending will accept and appreciate this cultural change.

You may be surprised that your attendance will gradually begin to increase as you do at least two more things. When you are gathering information, only ask for what you will need and use. When you are at the top of your game, first-time guests will get a text from you Sunday afternoon: "Thanks for being with us today in church. We are looking forward to seeing you again." During the week, guests should receive a letter from the church and, around Friday, a phone call. Some churches drop by the guests' home for a thirty-second meeting and give them a small gift.

Expect your first-time guests to be there next week or at least in the next month. On the following Sunday, and for the next month, be sure to have a printed nametag for the first-time guests who attended the previous week. In your electronic spreadsheet, record what percentage of first-time guests return within the next month. You will begin to see an increase in the percentage of first-time guests who return. When your records indicate that 15–20 percent of first-time guests are coming back a second time in the first month, it is time to celebrate! If a first-time guest does not come back in the first month, send out the thirty-day letter. If your return rate is low, it is time to take action. Each week, evaluate why first-time guests might not return and try to improve.

Remember that God is even more excited about seeing your church grow than you are. God is a team builder. We see this in the Trinity itself. The triune God accomplishes things in perfect union. Generally, this is how God works. He calls someone to do a certain job—like when he called Noah, Abraham, Moses, David, Isaiah, the twelve disciples, the apostle Paul, and numerous other individuals in the Old and New Testament and beyond. Generally, that individual or group begins to gather other people to accomplish God's call for their lives. So it is with building a growing church. Each day, pray, look for, and ask other people to join you. You cannot do it well by yourself. Then, as your team begins to come together, work together to accomplish God's call.

Do not be happy with the *status quo*. Continually change things to make them better and more efficient. I find myself tweaking even a well-oiled machine. Periodically, review what you are doing. Ask yourself if what you are doing in a particular area is producing the results you seek. Once you feel you have a good organization, try to be great. If you hit a wall in your growth program, bring in a "secret shopper." Listen carefully to their first impressions. Above all, keep your heart tuned to the heart of God.

CHAPTER EIGHT

CONCLUSION

MOST GROWTH IS GRADUAL, sometimes with an occasional burst. In one church I pastored, getting to sixty in attendance took a long time but growth from sixty to one hundred happened quickly. The Bible talks about not becoming weary in doing well. Make realistic goals that you can reach in a reasonable amount of time. My goal was to net one person a week in attendance over a long period. It would mean that after a year, fifty more people would be attending the church. I did not reach that goal. The average turned out to a net of 2/3 of a person a week in attendance over time. The church went from twenty to seventy-five, but it took seventeen months. Over the next two years, the attendance went to one hundred and fifty. The church is still not netting one person a week, but they are seeing continual growth. The weekly growth chart readily reveals some ups and downs and, occasionally, some bursts in growth.

Many church growth books provide information on how to implement various programs to help the church grow. This book, however, did not focus on implementing programs but simply sought to illustrate that implementing a few church growth principles can result in church growth. I am personally committed to assisting small, plateaued, or declining churches experience growth. If I can help you in any way, do not hesitate to contact me.

You may contact me at the following:
www.richardvarnell.com
richard@pdtax.com
Cell: 760-391-2954

SOURCES CONSULTED

Arn Win, and Charles Arn. *The Master's Plan for Making Disciples*. Monrovia, CA: Church Growth Press, 1982.

Arn, Win. *The Church Growth Ratio Book*. Pasadena, CA: Church Growth, 1987.

Barna, George. *How to Find Your Church*. Minneapolis, MN: Worldwide Publications, 1989.

Bilezikian, Gilbert. *Community 101: Reclaiming the Local Church as Community of Oneness*. Grand Rapids, MI: Zondervan, 1997.

Blanchard, Ken. *Raving Fans: A Revolutionary Approach to Customer Service*. New York, NY: William Morrow, 1993.

Bremer, Jill. "First Impression Power." Jill Bremer Executive Coaching. Accessed October 4, 2012. http://jillbremer.com/articles/communications/first-impression-power/

Carnegie, Dale. *How to Win Friends and Influence People*. New York, NY: Pocket Books/Simon & Schuster, 1981.

Chernow, Ron. *Titan: The Life of John D. Rockefeller Sr.* New York, NY: Vintage Books, 2004.

Clarensau, Mike. *From Belonging to Becoming: The Power of Loving People Like Jesus Did*. Springfield, MO: Influence, 2011.

Deming, W. Edwards. BrainyQuest.com. Accessed October 2, 2012. http://www.brainyquote.com/quotes/authors/w/w/_edwards_ deming.html.

Dolan, Tim "So, You Think You Are Friendly?" *Congregations* 38, no. 1 (2011): 14–18. Accessed September 29, 2012. ATLA Religion Database with ATLA Serials, EBCOhost.

Dudley, Carl S. *Where Have All Our People Gone?: New Choices for Old Churches*. New York, NY: The Pilgrim Press, 1979, 78.

Ekman, Paul, as quoted by Carlin Flora, "The Once-Over," *Psychology Today* (May/June 2004), Accessed August 18, 2007. http://psychologytoday.com/articles/pto-20040713-000004.html

Emerson, Ralph Waldo. *Essays: First and Second Series*. New York: Crowell, 1951.

Gainsbrugh, Jonathan. *Winning the Backdoor War: Growing Your Church by Closing its 7 Backdoors*. Elk Grove, CA: Harvest Church, 1993.

Gallup George Jr., *The People's Religion*. New York, NY: MacMillan, 1989.

George, Carl F. *How to Break Growth Barriers*. Grand Rapids, MI: Baker Book House, 1993.

Gorman, Julie A. *Community That Is Christian: A Handbook on Small Groups*. Wheaton, IL: Victor Books, 1993.

Hybels, Bill. *Courageous Leadership*. Grand Rapids, MI: Zondervan, 2002.

Jones, Laurie Beth. *Teach Your Team to Fish: Using Ancient Wisdom for Inspired Teamwork*. New York, NY: Three Rivers Press, 2002.

Khare, Shweta L. "Interview or Meeting—First Impression." Career Bright. Accessed October 4, 2012. http://careerbright.com/tag/you-only-have-one-chance-to-make-a-first-impression

Knight, Walter B. *Knight's Treasury of Illustrations*. Grand Rapids, MI: Eerdmans, 1963.

Longfellow, Henry Wadsworth. Living Life Fully. Accessed October 23, 2012. http://www.livinglifefully.com/thinkers longfellow.html

McGinnis, Alan Loy. *The Friendship Factor*. Minneapolis, MN: Augsburg Publishing House, 1979.

McIntosh Gary, and Glen Martin. *Finding Them, Keeping Them: Effective Strategies for Evangelism and Assimilation in the Local Church*. Nashville, TN: Broadman & Holman, 1992.

McIntosh, Gary L. *There's Hope for Your Church: First Steps to Restoring Health and Growth*. Grand Rapids: Baker Books, 2012.

McIntosh, Gary L. *Beyond the First Visit: The Complete Guide to Connecting Guests to Your Church*. Grand Rapids, MI: Baker Books, 2006.

Oswald, Roy M. *Making Your Church More Inviting*. Herndon, VA: The Alban Institute, 1992.

Rainer, Thomas. *High Expectations: The Remarkable Secret for Keeping People in Your Church*. Nashville, TN: Broadman & Holman, 1999.

Frazee, Randy. *The Connecting Church: Beyond Small Groups to Authentic Community*. Grand Rapids, MI: Zondervan, 2001.

Searcy, Nelson, and Jennifer Dykes Henson. *Fusion: Turning First-Time Guests into Fully-Engaged Members of Your Church*. Ventura, CA: Gospel Light, 2007.

Stetzer, Ed. *Planting New Churches in a Postmodern Age*. Nashville, TN: Broadman & Holman, 2003.

Tan, Paul Lee. *Encyclopedia of 7700 Illustrations*. Rockville, MD: Assurance Publishers, 1979.

Tillapaugh, Frank R. *Unleashing the Church*. Ventura, CA: Regal Books, 1982.

Towns, Elmer, Ed Stetzer, and Warren Bird. *11 Innovations in the Local Church: How Today's Leaders Can Learn, Discern and Move into the Future*. Ventura, CA: Regal, 2007.

Waltz, Mark L. *First Impressions: Creating Wow Experiences in Your Church*. Loveland, CO: Group, 2005.

Wilson, Timothy D. *Stranger to Ourselves: Discovering the Adaptive Unconscious*. Cambridge, MA: Harvard University Press, 2002.

"World Population Growth History." Vaughn's Summaries. Accessed August 13, 2012. http://www.vaughns-1-pagers.com/history//world-population-growth.htm

INVITATION LETTER
TO PASTORS

Date

Dear Pastor,

I am working on a doctoral project at the Assemblies of God Theological Seminary. The title of my project is "Stimulating Church Growth through Scripturally Based Business Strategies: Targeting Churches Plateaued or Declining in Attendance." According to AG Vital Statistics for 2010, about 58 percent of our churches are declining in attendance or their attendance has plateaued. I believe God has helped me to develop a plan to assist churches in their desire to grow. I believe any church can experience a 3 to 5 percent growth by utilizing these practical ideas.

I am looking for four churches to implement these ideas. The plan is designed to be for a year; however, I will monitor it for three months, which will include a monthly visit from February through April 2012. While there is no cost to participate in the project, I will be looking for churches that can answer "yes" to the questions below.

If you are interested in being part of the project, I would be delighted to communicate with you. Please give me a call at 760-391-2954 or email me at Richard@pdtax.com. If you do not qualify for the project, but know someone that may, please feel free to pass this information on to them.

Your friend in ministry,

Richard G. Varnell, D. Min.

1. The church I pastor has less than two hundred people in attendance.
2. The church I pastor has either declined or plateaued in attendance for the past three years.
3. I have records that show the church's attendance and financial giving for the past three years.

PASTOR AND CHURCH PROFILE

Date: _____

Name: _____

HomeAddress:_____

Email: _____

Cell: _____

How long have you pastored your current church? _____

Your educational background: (Circle what applies):

> High School
>
> College: 1 2 3 4
>
> BA
>
> MA
>
> Doctorate

What subjects are your degrees in?_____

How many years have you held a ministerial credential? _____

Name of Church: _____

Address of Church: _____

_____

Church Website _____

How long has this church been in existence? _____

Attendance:

     Last year _____

     2nd Year _____

     3rd Year _____

Total income:

     Last year _____

     2nd Year _____

     3rd Year _____

CHURCH GROWTH BUSINESS CONCEPTS – CHURCH GROWTH PROPOSAL FOR CHURCHES UNDER 200

THE FOLLOWING PROGRAM IS designed for churches with an average attendance of two hundred or less in their Sunday morning service. According to AG U.S. Vital Statistics 2010, about 84 percent of churches average under two hundred—64 percent less than one hundred and 36 percent under fifty. About 18 percent of churches are plateaued, 42 percent grew by one or more, and 40 percent declined by one or more. Christians who are entrusted by God to administrate his church should use all available resources to do the very best job possible (Luke 16:8). If your church is not growing, this program will generally produce a 3 to 5 percent growth annually. Follow this program for one year. Measure the results. Track the last three years of attendance and income. Based on that, project what your next twelve months should be. Implement the following program prayerfully and see the growth that God has intended. This program, when properly implemented, is designed to take one to two hours a week of the pastor's time.

I. **Telephone**

   A. Staff the office, with volunteers, if necessary, to answer the phone during normal business hours (8 a.m.–5 p.m. M–F).

   B. Employ a professional answering service to answer your telephone twenty-four hours a day, seven days a week when you are not in the office. They will screen your calls and pass on to you the calls that need the most urgent attention. The cost is usually about $100 a month. Make sure the pastor, or another responsible person, answers the phones, especially from Saturday noon through the end of the morning worship time. This can be done by forwarding the church phone to a cell phone. This is the time when most people call the church for directions or service times for the Sunday morning service. Engage, if possible, the inquirer on the telephone. Introduce yourself; find out their name and something about them. Then ask them to introduce themselves to you when they come to church.

II. **Finances**

   A. When receiving the offering, publicly ensure that it is obvious to all that the funds are being handled by people unrelated to staff and that the funds are safely guarded.

B. Giving is an important part of worship. The importance of giving should generally be emphasized by the pastor.

- The funds are used to bring people to Jesus.
- Giving is an act of worship and visitors should not be excluded.

The pastor can prepare at least a minute or two of devotion about giving before the offering is received. There are books that give suggestions for fifty-two weeks of biblical instruction regarding giving. Restricting giving to a certain group of people or to a particular fund may hinder the Holy Spirit from pouring out his blessings on the entire church. God's people are always blessed when they generously give to his work. For special projects, let the people see what they are giving to. For example, let the church send the entire youth group to youth camp. Bring the youth up before and after camp. The same can be done for children, missionaries, building fund, etc. Some people in each service want to give more than their tithes. They are waiting for the pastor to challenge them.

1. Occasionally, have a testimony (live or video) using someone who has been blessed by giving.

2. It is imperative to have proper accounting methods and segregation of duties when managing all the finances of the church.

3. Set up your accounting software to recognize first-time contributors. Send them a welcome from the church and recognize any offering they gave. This is also important for second- and third-time visitors.

4. Give a contribution report every three months as opposed to just once a year. This alone may increase the giving to the church by up to 6 percent.

5. Have the previous year's financial statements publicly available. There are great programs that can display the financial reports so that they are easily understood.

6. Have monthly financial statements for each board meeting that show current, year-to-date, and at least the previous year's records for comparison.

7. Teach a series using the book *The Blessed Life.*

III. **Attendance**

A. Use nametags for everyone. Print nametags ahead of time for regular attendees. Be sure that your "attendance table" is well staffed. Nametags that were left over will usually indicate those who were absent.

B. Take attendance each week. There are at least five ways to determine who attended your Sunday morning worship service with almost a 100 percent accuracy rate:

1. Ushers should take a head count of people in the main sanctuary, along with a count of those meeting at the same time in other areas of the church campus.
2. Each week, print out an attendance list of attendees for the previous week. Highlight recent visitor's names so that those at the "attendance table" may be able to greet them by name. As people receive their nametags, check off their names.
3. Before receiving the offering, have an attendance book with sign-in sheets at the end of each row and encourage everyone to sign in.
4. Have sign-in sheets for adults and children involved in children's activities.
5. Use the giving record as another source to determine who attended the worship service.

C. I use Excel to track names, addresses, phone numbers, email addresses, birthdays, anniversaries, and age categories, as well as track attendance each week.

D. No later than Monday, prepare a plan for the best way to contact the "regulars" who were absent.

E. Also, have a plan to contact first-, second-, and third-time attendees. You may want to use professionally written letters for this purpose. First, you may send out a letter or email, then a phone call. If you want an 80 percent return rate, take a small gift of bread, cookies, etc. around Friday or Saturday to their home. Spend no more than thirty seconds at their door. If they are not home, leave the gift and a personal note. Also, be sure to have special postcards for children that visit. Children's teachers should also telephone visitors. On your visitor cards, ask a question about how that person knew about your church. Capitalize on that information.

IV. **Communications**

A. Have a website for your church and update it weekly.

B. Build an email list to communicate quickly with the church family. Use it weekly.

C. Around Friday or Saturday once a month, or at least once a quarter, the pastor should telephone each family that regularly attends and take prayer requests. This permits the pastor to stay in contact with each family and often generates information not normally available. The church can use the information to effectively minister to that family.

V. **Create "Community" each Sunday morning:**

A. Have coffee and refreshments available before, during, or after the Sunday morning worship. Some churches take a seven- to ten-minute "break" after the offering is received and encourage everyone to fellowship. This is also a great time for the pastor and staff to greet visitors as well as regulars.

B. Take time to greet visitors and encourage them to complete the visitor information card. If there are special visitors, introduce them at this time.

C. Once a month, provide a meal following the worship service at no cost. This could be pizza from Costco or Sam's, hamburgers and hot dogs, sandwiches, etc.

D. Have enough ushers to seat people who arrive late, and to escort visitors and their children to the children's place of worship.

E. Have outings every month or two for the seniors.

F. Add one or two positions to your board for people from outside your church to give you that extra set of eyes.

G. Send postcards to people with birthdays or anniversaries approaching; even better, make a personal telephone call to them on the actual date of celebration.

H. At least annually, have a member appreciation event.

I. Some churches follow the "three-minute rule," which means regulars are encouraged to greet visitors following the Sunday morning service for at least three minutes before they visit with friends.

GETTING TO KNOW YOU ... (A LITTLE BETTER) CARD

Date: _____

Name: _____ _____
                              Last   *First*

Spouse's Name: _____

Street Address: _____

City/State/Zip: _____ _____ _____

Home Phone: _____

☐ Single   ☐ Married   Anniversary: _____ /_____ /_____
                                         Month   Day   Year

☐ Member   **☐ Regular Attender**   **☐ Visitor**

FIRST PERSON

Email: _____ Phone: _____

Birthdate: _____ /_____ /_____
           Month   Day   Year

SPOUSE

Email: _____ Phone: _____

Birthdate: _____ /_____ /_____
           Month   Day   Year

Children At Home:

Name: _____ Birthdate: _____ /_____ /_____

Name: _____ Birthdate: _____ /_____ /_____

Name: _____ Birthdate: _____ /_____ /_____

Name: _____ Birthdate: _____ /_____ /_____

WELCOME CARD
(FRONT AND BACK)

WELCOME!

Date: _____

Name(s): _____   _____

Address: _____

City/State/Zip: _____

Email: _____ Status: ☐Single   ☐Married

Phone: _____ Spouse Phone:_____

Birthday: _____ /_____   **Spouse's Birthday:** _____ /_____
         Month   *Year*   *Month*   *Year*

Children:

Name:_____ Birthdate: ___/___/___ Name: _____ Birthdate: ___/___/___

Name:_____ Birthdate: ___/___/___ Name: _____ Birthdate: ___/___/___

1st / 2nd / 3rd time visitor   ☐ Regular Attendee   ☐ Member

I would like more information on...

☐ Becoming a Christian   ☐ Being baptized   ☐ Becoming a Member

I was invited by: _____

How did you hear about us?_____

BACK

I would like more information on...

☐ Small Groups ☐ Service Groups
☐ Counseling ☐ Children's Ministry
☐ Volunteering ☐ Youth Ministries
☐ Singles Ministries ☐ Senior Ministries

Prayer Requests/Comments:

_____

_____

_____

_____

_____

_____

SAMPLE "MISSING IN ACTION" (MIA) LETTER

Date

Dear

We missed you!

If there is anything that we can do to be a blessing, please let us know. My personal email is pastorvarnell@gmail.com or you can reach me on my cell phone at (760) 391-2954. We have many tools at our disposal to help in times of need. My goal, as your pastor, is to be a blessing you.

I pray you are having a blessed week. Please, let me know if there is anything I can do to be of assistance.

Warmly,

Matthew Varnell
Senior Pastor

APPENDIX G

SAMPLE FIRST-TIME GUEST LETTER (WITH CONTRIBUTION)

Date

First-Time Guest,

Dear First-Time Guest,

I am thrilled you chose to visit us at Desert MultiChurch this past weekend! It has been my experience over the years that God often has a specific reason for bringing people to visit our church. Perhaps it was a timely message they needed to hear, or perhaps they were or are at a point of need in their lives. Maybe a family member, friend, or co-worker invited them. Whatever the reason for your visit, I am so glad you came. We are committed to being responsive to any needs that you or your family may have. We are dedicated in all that we do to provide an atmosphere where people can grow closer to God and to each other.

I also want to say that we truly desire to meet your needs and the needs of your family. Please let us know if there is any way we can better serve you.

I also want to thank you for your contribution of $100.

Lastly, I'd like to invite you to join us again this weekend at our 10:00 a.m. Sunday service. If you have any questions about our church or about the many ministries we offer, please feel free to call the church office. I hope to see you again this weekend!

God Bless You!

Richard Varnell
Senior Pastor

SAMPLE FIRST-TIME GUEST LETTER

Date

First-Time Guest,

Dear First-Time Guest,

I am thrilled you chose to visit us at Desert MultiChurch this past weekend! It has been my experience over the years that God often has a specific reason for bringing people to visit our church. Perhaps it was a timely message they needed to hear, or perhaps they were or are at a point of need in their lives. Maybe a family member, friend, or co-worker invited them. Whatever the reason for your visit, I am so glad you came. We are committed to being responsive to any needs that you or your family may have. We are dedicated in all that we do to provide an atmosphere where people can grow closer to God and to each other.

I also want to say that we truly desire to meet your needs and the needs of your family. Please let us know if there is any way we can better serve you.

Lastly, I'd like to invite you to join us again this weekend at our 10:00 a.m. Sunday service. If you have any questions about our church or about the many ministries we offer, please feel free to call the church office. I hope to see you again this weekend!

God Bless You!

Richard Varnell
Senior Pastor

SAMPLE SECOND-TIME GUEST LETTER

Date

Second-Time Guest
Street
City, State Zip

Dear Second-Time Guest,

I was delighted that you chose to visit us again at Desert MultiChurch! I hope this means that you were pleased with your first visit. If you are looking for a church home, I understand that it can be a challenging process, as it is one of the most important decisions you will make for you and your family.

Whatever your circumstances, I am committed to helping you connect with lifelong friends and find a place where you can spiritually grow and express your gifts and talents. The passion of our church is to see you realize all of God's purposes for your life and to develop into the full potential of what he has for you.

If I can help in any way, please feel free to give me a call this week.

Thank you again for giving us the opportunity to minister to you and your family. I look forward to seeing you at church next Sunday.

God bless you,

Matthew Varnell
Senior Pastor

SAMPLE THIRD-TIME GUEST LETTER

Dear Third-Time Guest,

I want to personally thank you for joining us once again at Rock House Community Church. I would like you and your family to feel free to take advantage of all the resources we make available to our attendees and members. I want you to know that as life happens, I or one of our caring staff will always be available for counseling, prayer, hospital visitation, or anything else you might need.

I would like to personally invite you to attend our next Membership 101 class. It's not just about becoming a member (though we would be honored should you decide to join) but is a tremendous resource describing who we are and what we are about. Our next Membership 101 will be next Sunday, September 11, immediately following the 11 a.m. service. Childcare will be provided as well as lunch, on us! You may sign up by checking the appropriate box on your welcome card, by calling our office, or stopping by the information center before or after any of our weekend services. I look forward to seeing you there!

If you are new or returning to church attendance, I would like to encourage you to do three things:

a. Buy and read a One-Year Bible (available at our store, your local Christian Bookstore, or Amazon).

b. Take fifteen minutes every morning to pray before you get going for the day.

c. Make a friend from church. Go to a small group, attend a football party, volunteer to usher, or help in a children's class. Whatever you enjoy doing, find a way to do it with a new friend from church.

Again, thank you for joining us again at Rock House Community Church. I look forward to being a friend and your pastor for many years to come.

Warmly,

Matthew Varnell
Senior Pastor

SAMPLE SECOND-TIME GUEST LETTER (WITH CONTRIBUTION)

Date

Second-Time Guest

Dear Second-Time Guest,

I was delighted that you chose to visit us again at Desert MultiChurch! I hope this means that you were pleased with your first visit. If you are looking for a church home, I understand that it can be a challenging process, as it is one of the most important decisions you will make for you and your family.

Whatever your circumstances, I am committed to helping you connect with lifelong friends and to find a place where you can spiritually grow and express your gifts and talents. The passion of our church is to see you realize all of God's purposes for your life and to develop into the full potential of what he has for you.

I also want to thank you for your contribution of $100. If I can help in any way, please feel free to give me a call this week.

Thank you again for giving us the opportunity to minister to you and your family. I look forward to seeing you at church next Sunday.

God bless you,

Matthew Varnell
Senior Pastor

SAMPLE THIRD-TIME GUEST LETTER (WITH CONTRIBUTION)

Date

Dear Third-Time Guest,

I want to personally thank you for joining us once again at Rock House Community Church. I would like you and your family to feel free to take advantage of all the resources we make available to our attendees and members. I want you to know that as life happens, I or one of our caring staff will always be available for counseling, prayer, hospital visitation, or anything else you might need.

I would like to personally invite you to attend our next Membership 101 class. It's not just about becoming a member (though we would be honored should you decide to join) but is a tremendous resource describing who we are and what we are about. Our next Membership 101 will be next Sunday, September 11, immediately following the 11 a.m. service. Childcare will be provided as well as lunch, on us! You may sign up by checking the appropriate box on your welcome card, by calling our office, or stopping by the information center before or after any of our weekend services. I look forward to seeing you there!

If you are new or returning to church attendance, I would like to encourage you to do three things:

1. Buy and read a One-Year Bible (available at our store, local Christian Bookstore, or Amazon).
2. Take fifteen minutes every morning to pray before you get going for the day.
3. Make a friend from church. Go to a small group, attend a football party, volunteer to usher, or help in a children's class. Whatever you enjoy doing, find a way to do it with a new friend from church.

I also want to thank you for your contribution of $100. Again, thank you for joining us again at Rock House Community Church. I look forward to being a friend and your pastor for many years to come.

Warmly,

Matthew Varnell
Senior Pastor

SAMPLE THIRTY-DAY FOLLOW-UP LETTER

Date

First-Time Guest
Street
City, State Zip

Dear First-Time Guest,

   I appreciate you visiting Desert Assembly of God for the first time last month. I hope that you found our church both friendly and able to meet your spiritual needs. I want everyone who attends Desert Assembly of God to have a wonderful worship experience and to find a personal encounter with God.

   If you are interested in meeting new people, I want to invite you to a special lunch we are having this next Sunday following our morning worship service. We will be meeting at noon and this would be an opportunity for me to meet you personally. I hope that you will be able to attend.

Please have a wonderful week, and I look forward to seeing you soon. Please feel free to give me a call if you should have any questions.

May God's good blessings be with you!

Yours most sincerely,

Richard Varnell
Senior Pastor

P.S. I have enclosed a music CD that I think you will enjoy.

SAMPLE "THANK YOU FOR GIVING" LETTER

Date

Richard and Joy Varnell

Dear Richard and Joy,

I just wanted to drop you a note to say thanks. It came to our attention that you gave to Newport Mesa for the first time this year. As I'm sure you understand, we track people who invest in God's work through Newport-Mesa so that we can provide quarterly and year-end contribution statements for tax purposes.

What a powerful step of faith for you to take! I don't know how much you invested, but God does, and he promises blessings as we faithfully invest in building his kingdom (Luke 6:38; Malachi 3:10; Matthew 6:19).

My wife, Julie, and I have found it amazing to see how God has honored our faithfulness in giving back to Him. We have come to understand two things with striking clarity. First, we can't out give God. Second, giving has become an exciting adventure for us.

I'm excited for you as you continue your adventure of investing in God's work.

Blessings,

Scott Rachels

Church Growth—Take Your temperature

Usually, we go see the doctor for one of two reasons. We are either not feeling well, or we go to get a checkup. This is called preventative medicine. In either case, the doctor almost always checks your temperature and other vital signs. If we are sick, we may need to do healthy things to become well again. The church is similar. If your church attendance is staying even or growing, you may want to do things a little better to improve its health. If your church attendance is declining, you may need to look harder to reverse the downward trend. For either our physical bodies or the church, improved knowledge is beneficial.

Now it is time to check your church's "vital" signs. Answer each of the questions below. If your church is off track a little, answering these questions may help you get on track again. If you are already on track, these questions may help you roll down the road a little faster. Once you finish, send in your responses and receive a complimentary health evaluation (Richard@ptax.com).

Circle the answer that most accurately reflects your church or fill in the requested information.

I. Size of Buildings

A. Do you meet in temporary or permanent facilities?

B. Sanctuary or Sunday morning meeting place

1. Square footage _____
2. Type of seats—Fixed or movable
3. Type of floor—flat or sloped
4. Seating capacity _____
5. Is building handicap accessible? _____
6. If 10 percent of your attendance was handicapped, could they find a place to sit? _____
7. Are restrooms handicap equipped? _____

C. Children Buildings

1. Nursery (0–3)
   a. Square footage _____
   b. At twenty square feet per child, what is your nursery capacity? ____
2. Children (age 4 – grade 6)
   a. Square footage_____
   b. At fifteen square feet per child, what is your children's area capacity? ____

D. Parking Lot

1. Is the parking lot paved? _____

    2. Is the parking lot striped? _____

    3. Number of parking spaces _____

    4. Number of handicap parking spaces _____

    5. Are there any "special" parking spaces marked "First-Time Guests" near the front of the entrance to the worship center? _____ If so, how many? _____

II. Attendance

A. Do you keep an accurate count of your attendance each week? _____

B. Attendance average this year _____

C. Attendance average last year _____

D. Attendance average year before last _____

E. Do you know each person in attendance by name and record their attendance each week? _____

F. Do you have a way to track first-time guests to check if they come back in the next month? _____

G. Do you measure your assimilation rate to see if first-time guests become second-time attendees? _____

H. Do you have nametags for each person attending the service? _____

I. How do you find out who are first-time guests?

    1. Do you have welcome cards? _____

    2. Are welcome cards and pens given to first-time guests when they walk in the door? _____

3. Are there welcome cards and pens for each person attending your services? _____

4. How do you encourage first-time guests to turn in their welcome cards?

_____

_____

_____

_____

_____

5. Do you provide a gift to first-time guests? _____ If so, what is the gift? _____

_____

6. Do you provide coffee and snacks before service to all who attend? _____

7. Do you have a meet and greet time during the service? _____

8. Is there a formal place for meeting first-time guests following the service? _____

J. Greeters and Ushers

1. Are people greeted when they enter the parking lot? _____

2. Are people greeted before they enter the building? _____

3. Are people greeted after they enter the building? _____

4. Do you have ushers who can help people find a seat? _____

     5. Do you have greeters to greet each person as they leave the service? _____

III. Follow-up

A. Do you give a time for commitment for salvation each week? _ _____

B. Following the time of commitment, do you have a way to get contact information from those who respond? _____

C. Do you have a specific follow-up plan for those who responded to the altar call to be enrolled in a course? _____

D. Do you send first-time guests an email within twenty-four hours? _____

E. Do you send first-time guests a letter during the week? _____

F. Do first-time guests receive a phone call during the week? _____

G. Do you prepare a nametag for first-time guests for the next Sunday? _____

H. Do you have a way for first-, second-, and third-time guests to join a small group or to become active in a ministry position? _____

I. After a person has attended three times, do you have a face-to-face meeting with them over coffee or a meal to access how they might fit into the church? _____

IV. Training

A. Do you have a monthly leadership training program where you provide a meal and childcare? _____

B. Do you provide training for each person serving in an official capacity? _____

V. Finances

A. Do you say some encouraging words about giving each Sunday before the offering is received? _____

B. Do you give people an opportunity to give to a special project each week besides the general fund? _____

C. Do you send out quarterly giving statements with a letter from the pastor expressing thankfulness and casting vision? _____

D. Do you have connections with a local Christian attorney who may help those who want a will, trust, or to give stocks or property? _____

ENDNOTES

1. Gilbert Bilezikian, Community 101: Reclaiming the Local Church as Community of Oneness (Grand Rapids, MI: Zondervan, 1997), 19.
2. Bilezikian, 15.
3. Mike Clarensau, *From Belonging to Becoming: The Power of Loving People Like Jesus Did* (Springfield, MO: Influence, 2011), 125.
4. Julie A. Gorman, *Community That Is Christian: A Handbook on Small Groups* (Wheaton, IL: Victor Books, 1993), 50.
5. "World Population Growth History," Vaughn's Summaries, accessed August 13, 2012, http://www.vaughns-1-pagers.com/history//world-population-growth.htm
6. Clarensau, 124.
7. Ron Chernow, *Titan: The Life of John D. Rockefeller Sr.* (New York, NY: Vintage Books, 2004), 46.
8. Ibid.
9. Thomas Rainer, *Autopsy of a Deceased Church* (Nashville, TN: Broadman & Holman, 2014), 7.
10. Gary L. McIntosh, *Beyond the First Visit: The Complete Guide to Connecting Guests to Your Church* (Grand Rapids, MI: Baker Books, 2006).
11. Carl F. George, *How to Break Growth Barriers* (Grand Rapids, MI: Baker Book House, 1993), 51.
12. Ibid., 137.
13. George, 139.
14. Clarensau, 12–13.
15. Tim Dolan, "So, You Think You are Friendly?" *Congregations* 38, no. 1 (2011): 14–18, accessed September 29, 2012, ATLA Religion Database with ATLA Serials, EBCOhost.
16. Dolan, "So, You Think You Are Friendly?"
17. Nelson Searcy with Jennifer Dykes Henson, *Fusion: Turning First-Time Guests into Fully-Engaged Members of Your Church* (Ventura, CA: Gospel Light, 2007), 27.
18. W. Edwards Deming, BrainyQuest.com, accessed October 2, 2012, http://www.brainyquote.com/quotes/authors/w/w /_edwards_deming.html
19. Searcy, 69.
20. Clarensau, 177.
21. Dale Carnegie, *How to Win Friends and Influence People* (New York, NY: Pocket Books/Simon & Schuster, 1981), 246.
22. Roy M. Oswald, *Making Your Church More Inviting* (Herndon, VA: The Alban

Institute, 1992), 95–96.

23. Dolan, "So, You Think You Are Friendly?"

24. Laurie Beth Jones, *Teach Your Team to Fish: Using Ancient Wisdom for Inspired Teamwork* (New York, NY: Three Rivers Press, 2002), xvii-xviii.

25. George Gallup Jr., *The People's Religion* (New York, NY: MacMillan, 1989), 32.

26. Randy Frazee, *The Connecting Church: Beyond Small Groups to Authentic Community* (Grand Rapids, MI: Zondervan, 2001), 37.

27. Jonathan Gainsbrugh, *Winning the Backdoor War: Growing Your Church by Closing its 7 Backdoors* (Elk Grove, CA: Harvest Church, 1993), 98.

28. Ibid., 95–96.

29. Elmer Towns, Ed Stetzer, and Warren Bird, *11 Innovations in the Local Church: How Today's Leaders Can Learn, Discern and Move into the Future* (Ventura, CA: Regal, 2007), 226.

30. Bill Hybels, *Courageous Leadership* (Grand Rapids, MI: Zondervan, 2002), 55.

31. Ed Stetzer, *Planting New Churches in a Postmodern Age* (Nashville, TN: Broadman & Holman, 2003), 100.

32. Ibid.

33. Gary L. McIntosh, *There's Hope for Your Church: First Steps to Restoring Health and Growth* (Grand Rapids: Baker Books, 2012), 100.

34. Shweta L. Khare, "Interview or Meeting—First Impression," Career Bright, accessed October 4, 2012, http://careerbright.com/tag/you-only-have-one-chance-to-make-a-first-impression

35. Jill Bremer, "First Impression Power," Jill Bremer Executive Coaching, accessed October 4, 2012, http://jillbremer.com/articles/communications/first-impression-power/

36. Searcy, 49.

37. Jill Bremer, "First Impression Power."

38. Timothy D. Wilson, *Stranger to Ourselves: Discovering the Adaptive Unconscious* (Cambridge, MA: Harvard University Press, 2002), 18.

39. Mark L. Waltz, *First Impressions: Creating Wow Experiences in Your Church* (Loveland, CO: Group, 2005), 37.

40. Searcy, 54.

41. Waltz, 42.

42. McIntosh, *Beyond the First Visit*, 35.

43. Paul Ekman, quoted by Carlin Flora, "The Once-Over," *Psychology Today* (May/June 2004), accessed August 18, 2007, http://psychologytoday.com/articles/pto-200407 13-000004.html

44. Rainer, 82.

45. Ibid.

46. Searcy, 61.

47. Ken Blanchard, *Raving Fans: A Revolutionary Approach to Customer Service* (New York, NY: William Morrow, 1993), 100.

48. McIntosh, *Beyond the First Visit*, 133.

49. Rainer, 84.

50.	Ibid.
51.	Searcy, 86.
52.	Rainer, 93.
53.	Searcy, 93.
54.	Ibid., 94.
55.	Rainer, 94-95.
56.	Clarensau, 183.
57.	Searcy, 99.
58.	Thomas S. Argyle, personal interview with author, September 1988.
59.	Searcy, 105.
60.	Gainsbrugh, 104.
61.	Rainer, 170.
62.	Gary McIntosh and Glen Martin, *Finding Them, Keeping Them: Effective Strategies for Evangelism and Assimilation in the Local Church* (Nashville, TN: Broadman & Holman, 1992), 75–135.
63.	Ralph Waldo Emerson, Essays: First and Second Series (New York, NY: Crowell, 1951), 65.
64.	McIntosh and Martin, 75.
65.	Alan Loy McGinnis, *The Friendship Factor* (Minneapolis, MN: Augsburg Publishing House, 1979), 9.
66.	Win Arn and Charles Arn, *The Master's Plan for Making Disciples* (Monrovia, CA: Church Growth Press, 1982), 156.
67.	Carl S. Dudley, *Where Have All Our People Gone?: New Choices for Old Churches* (New York, NY: The Pilgrim Press, 1979), 78.
68.	George Barna, *How to Find Your Church* (Minneapolis, MN: Worldwide Publications, 1989), 93.
69.	Win Arn, *The Church Growth Ratio Book* (Pasadena, CA: Church Growth, 1987), 10.
70.	Frank R. Tillapaugh, *Unleashing the Church* (Ventura, CA: Regal Books, 1982), 78.
71.	McIntosh and Martin, 101.
72.	Ibid., 95.
73.	Charles Spurgeon, as quoted in McIntosh and Martin, 95.
74.	McIntosh and Martin, 96.
75.	Paul Lee Tan, *Encyclopedia of 7700 Illustrations* (Rockville, MD: Assurance Publishers, 1979), 192.
76.	Towns, Stetzer, and Bird, 162.
77.	Tan, 206.
78.	Walter B. Knight, *Knight's Treasury of Illustrations* (Grand Rapids, MI: Eerdmans, 1963), 357.
79.	Henry Wadsworth Longfellow, Living Life Fully, http://www.livinglifefully. com/thinkers longfellow.html (accessed October 23, 2012).